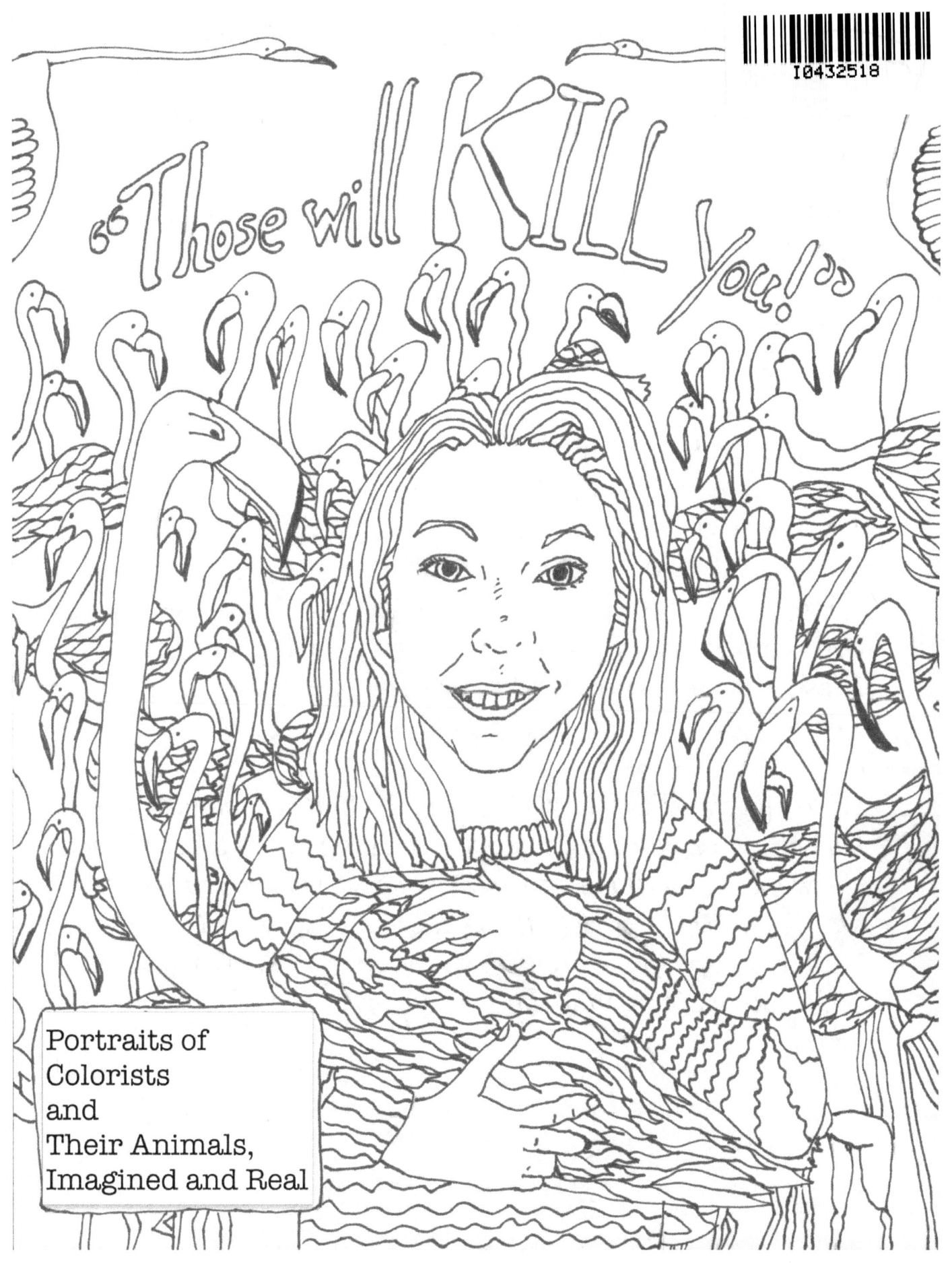

Those will KILL You!, Portraits of Colorists and Their Animals, Imagined and Real, by Artsy Fartsy Coloring, illustrated by Shoshanah Lee Marohn, Copyright ©2017 Shoshanah Lee Marohn, all rights reserved.

ISBN-13:
978-1979795302

ISBN-10:
1979795304

Cover art by Shoshanah Marohn and Zelma Marohn. Cover model is colorist Marilyn Reading. Back cover by Shoshanah Marohn. Back cover model is colorist Gina Wenzel-Garza.

No reprints of any pictures in this book, digital or physical, are permitted without the express written permission of Shoshanah Lee Marohn and Nature's First Green, LLC. Artsy Fartsy Coloring is a pen name for Shoshanah Lee Marohn.

Why is it called "Those Will KILL You"? Marilyn Reading's son believed flamingoes to be deadly dangerous animals, and when she went near to them once, when he was very young, he screamed, "Don't go near those, Mom! Those will KILL you!" The story inspired the drawing on the cover, which then inspired the creation of this entire book of portraits of colorists with animals.

"Animals don't lie. Animals don't criticize. If animals have moody days, they handle them better than humans do."

— Betty White

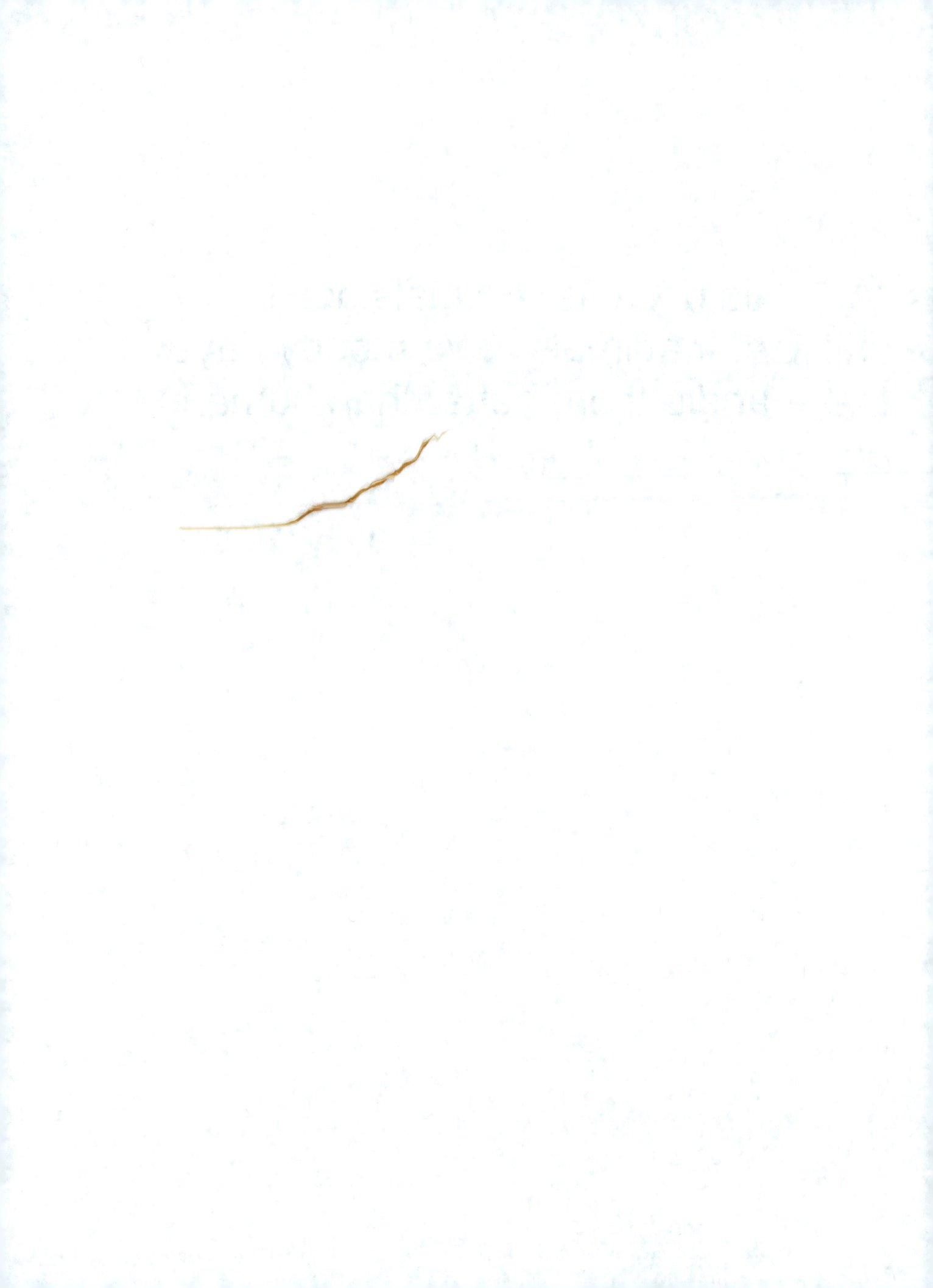

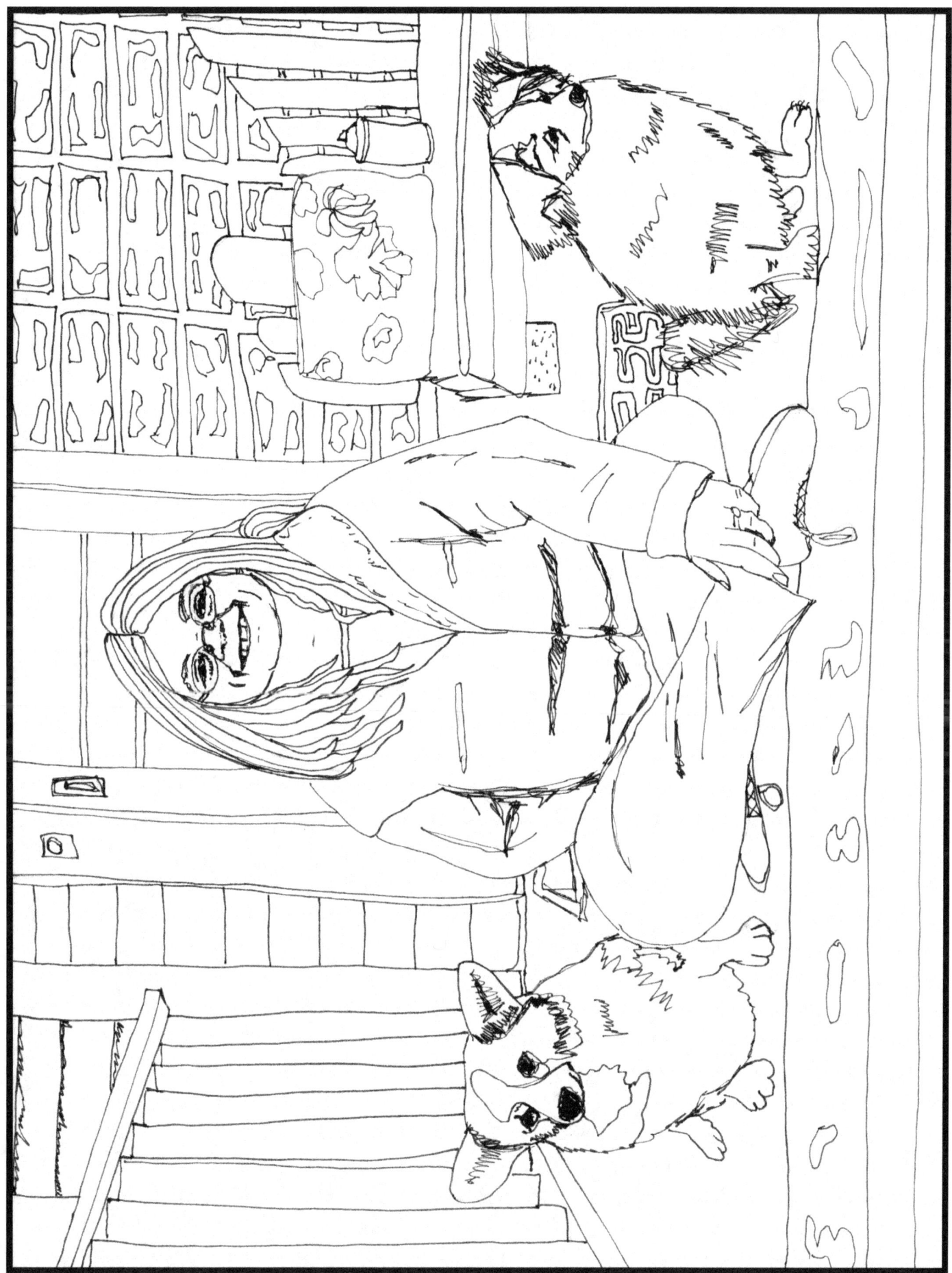

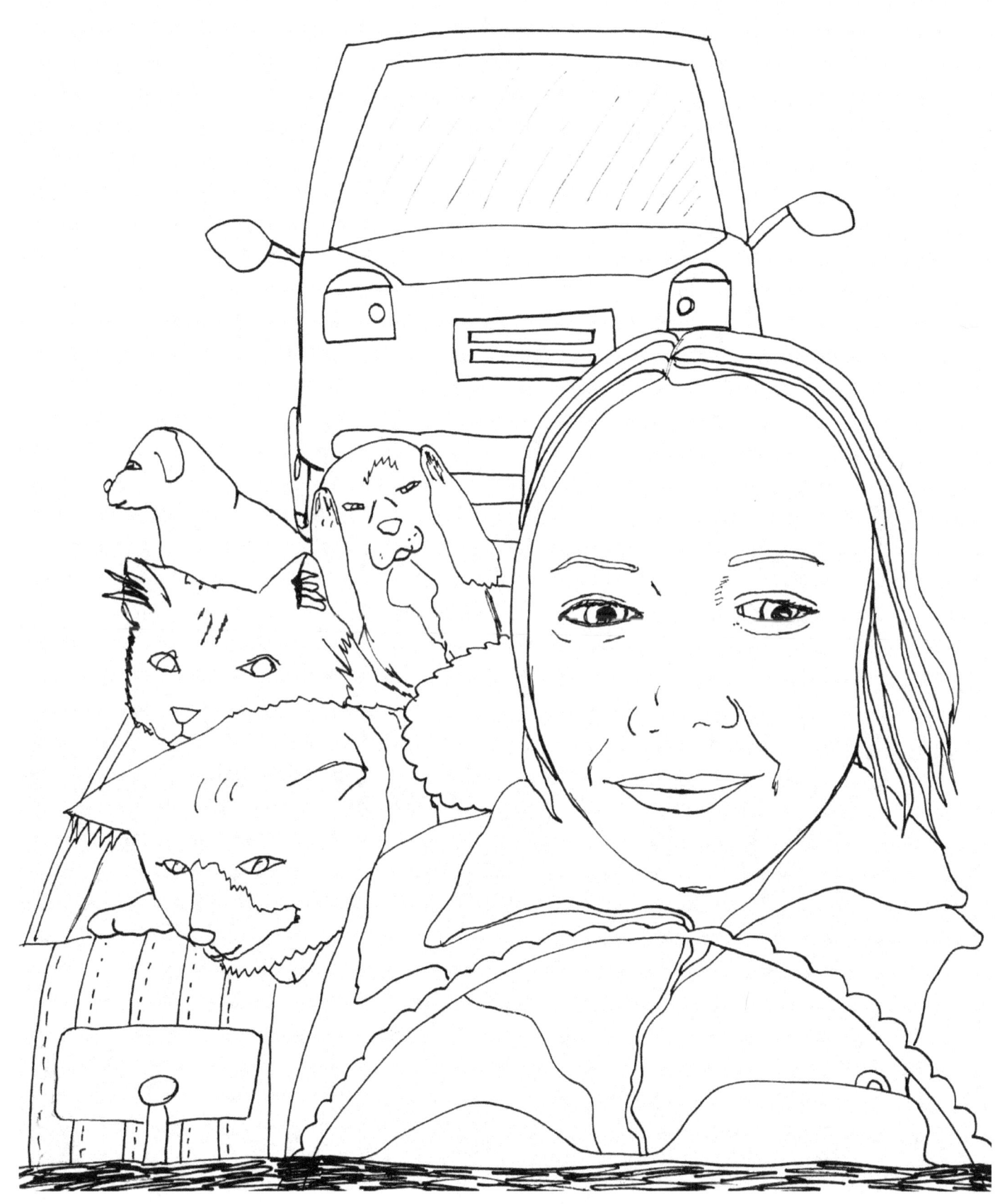

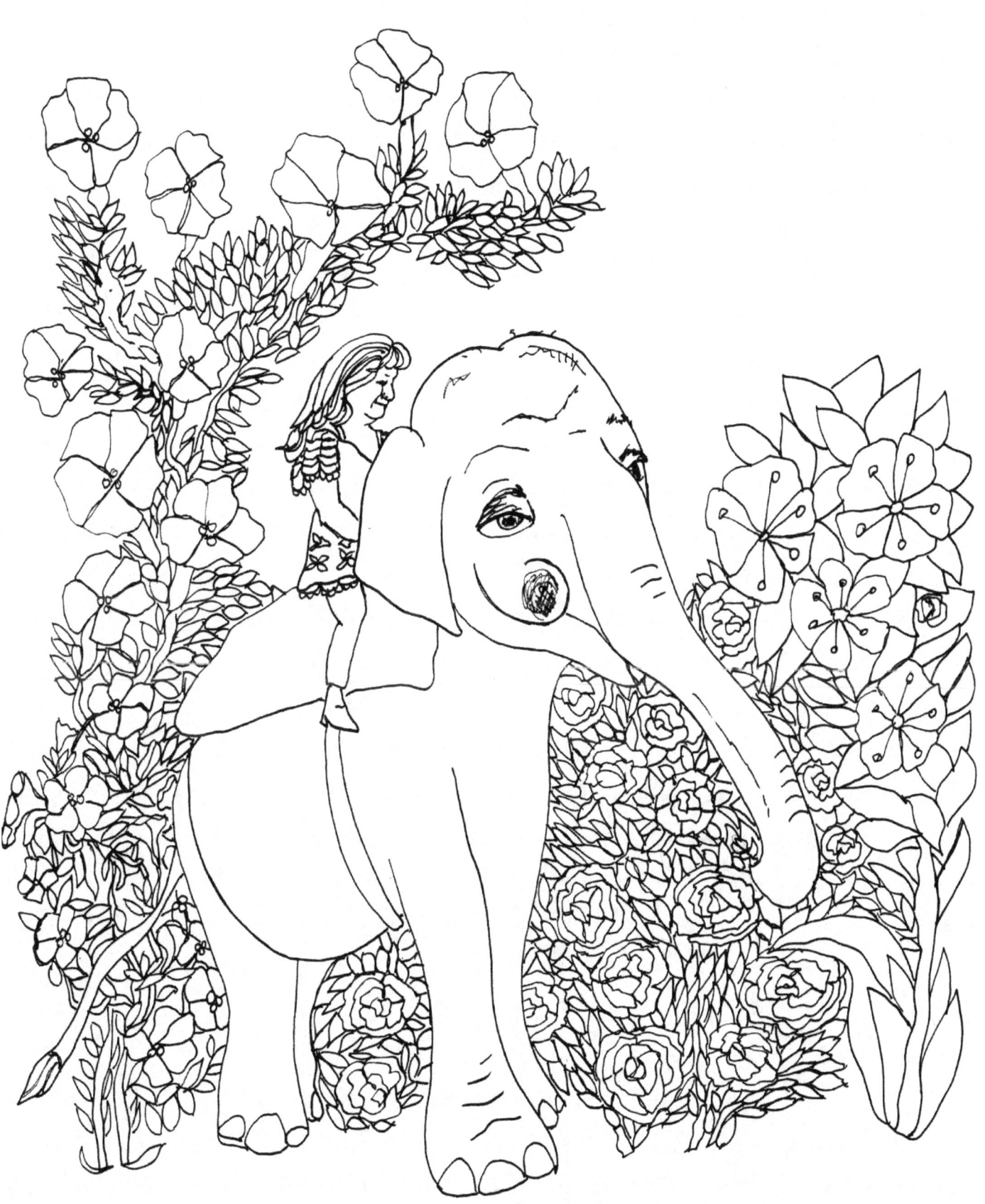

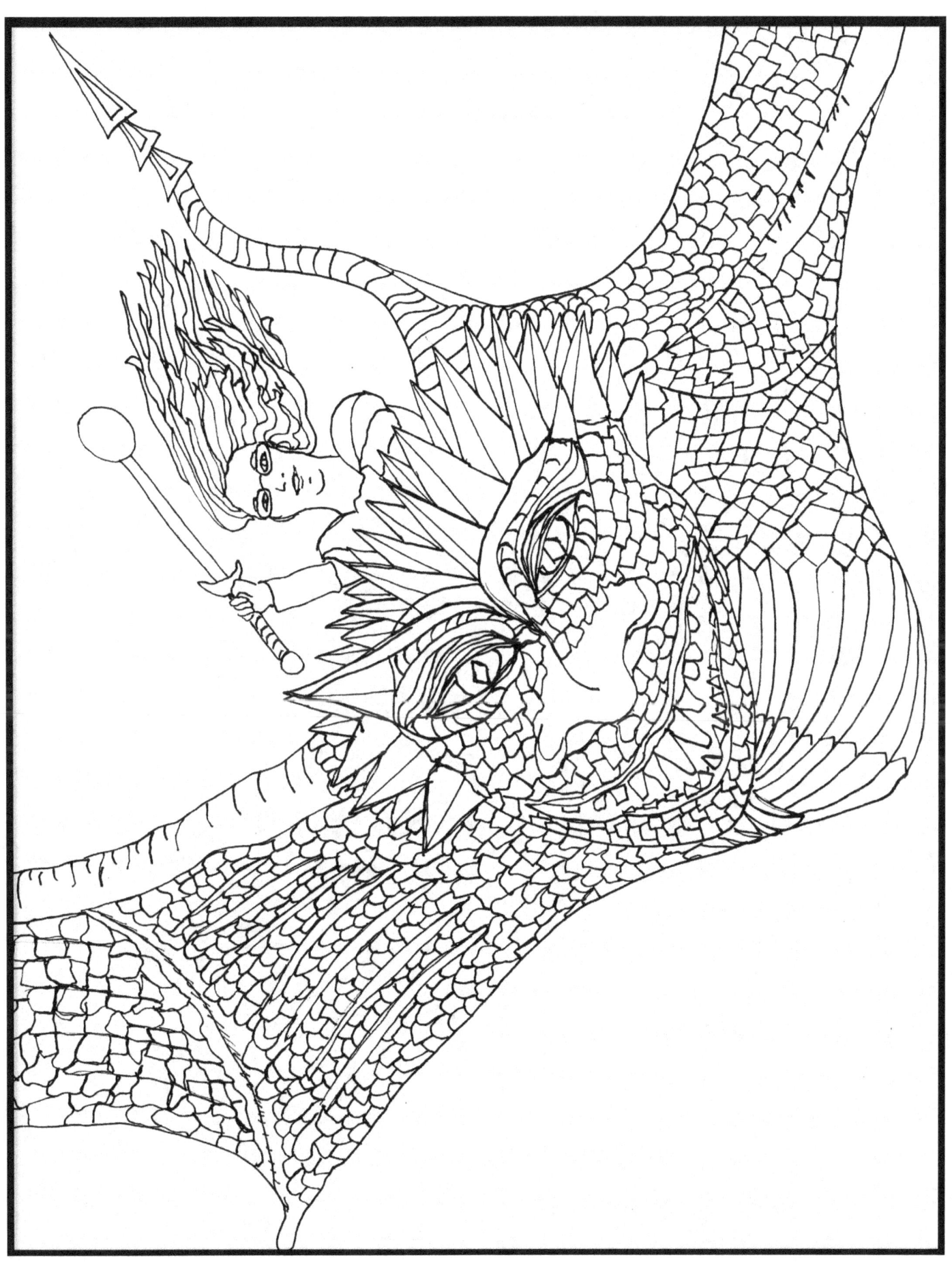

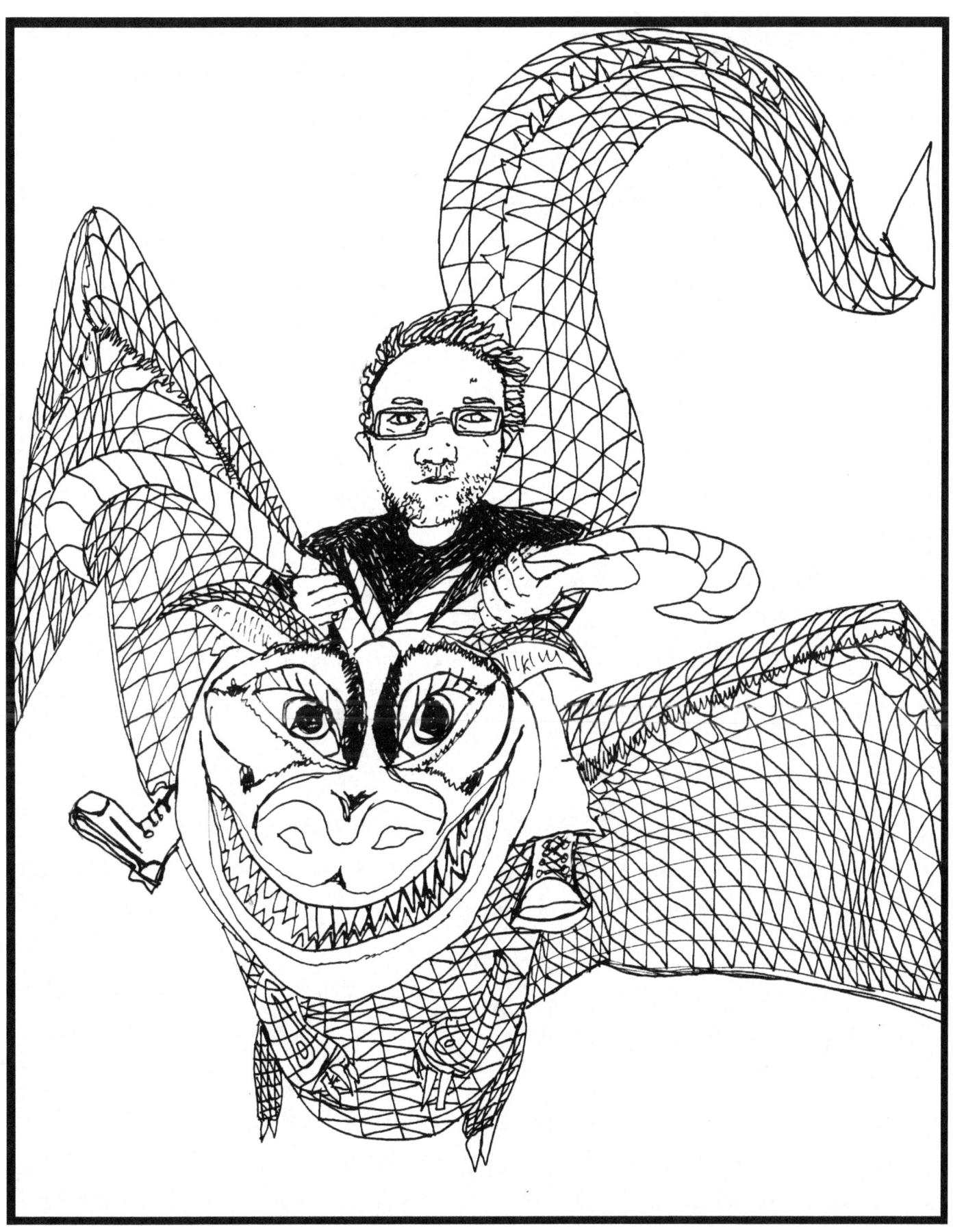

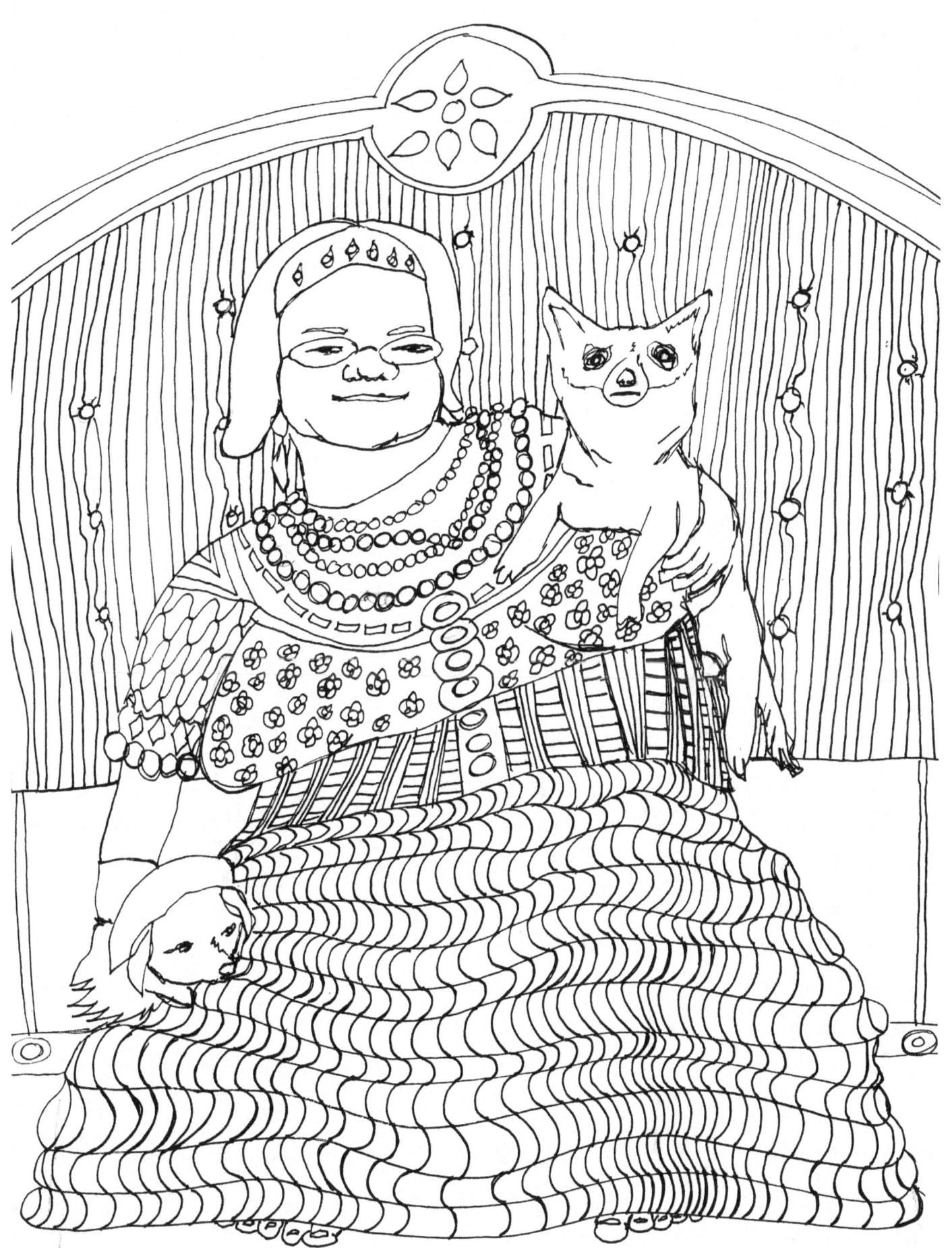

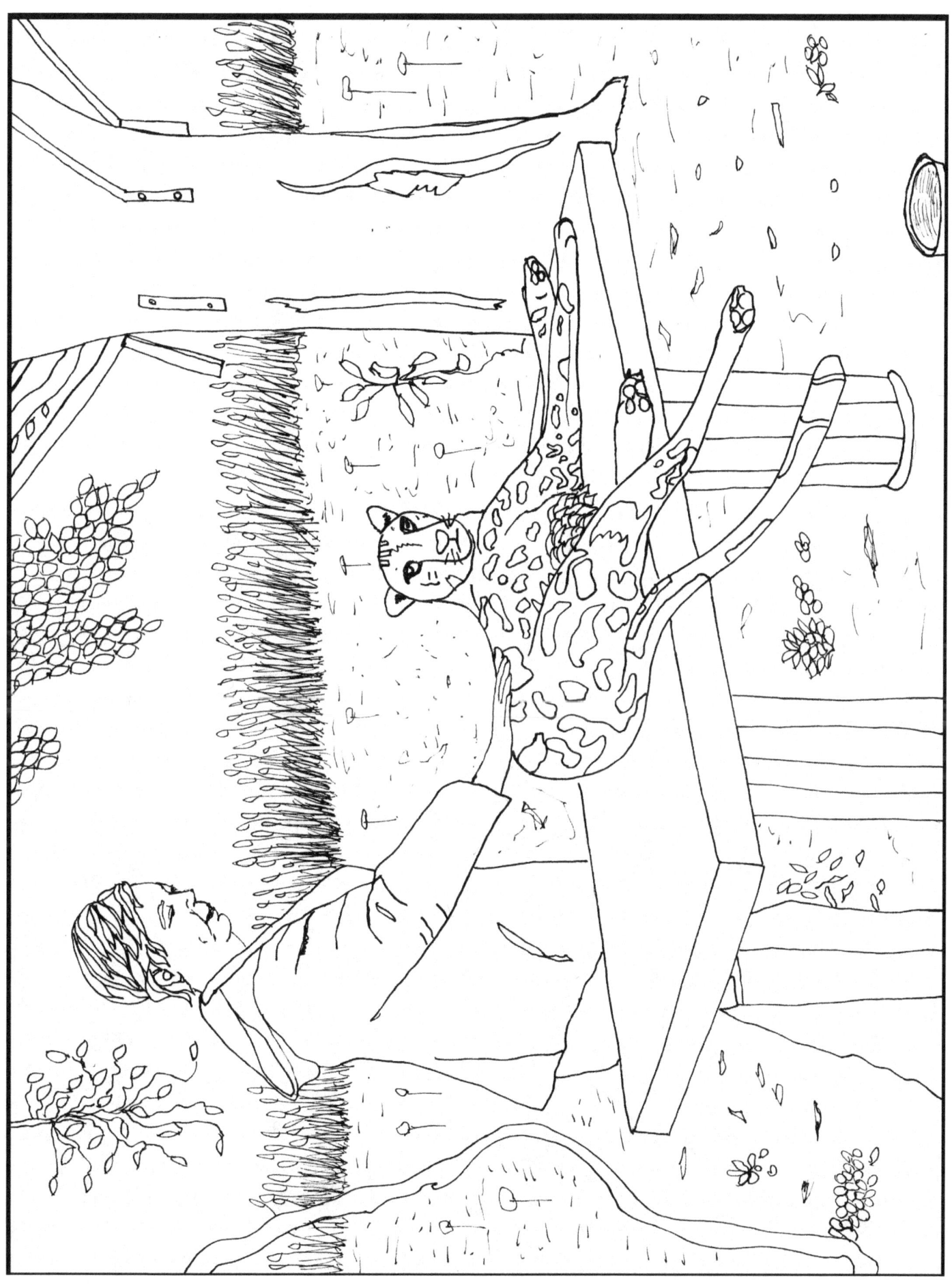

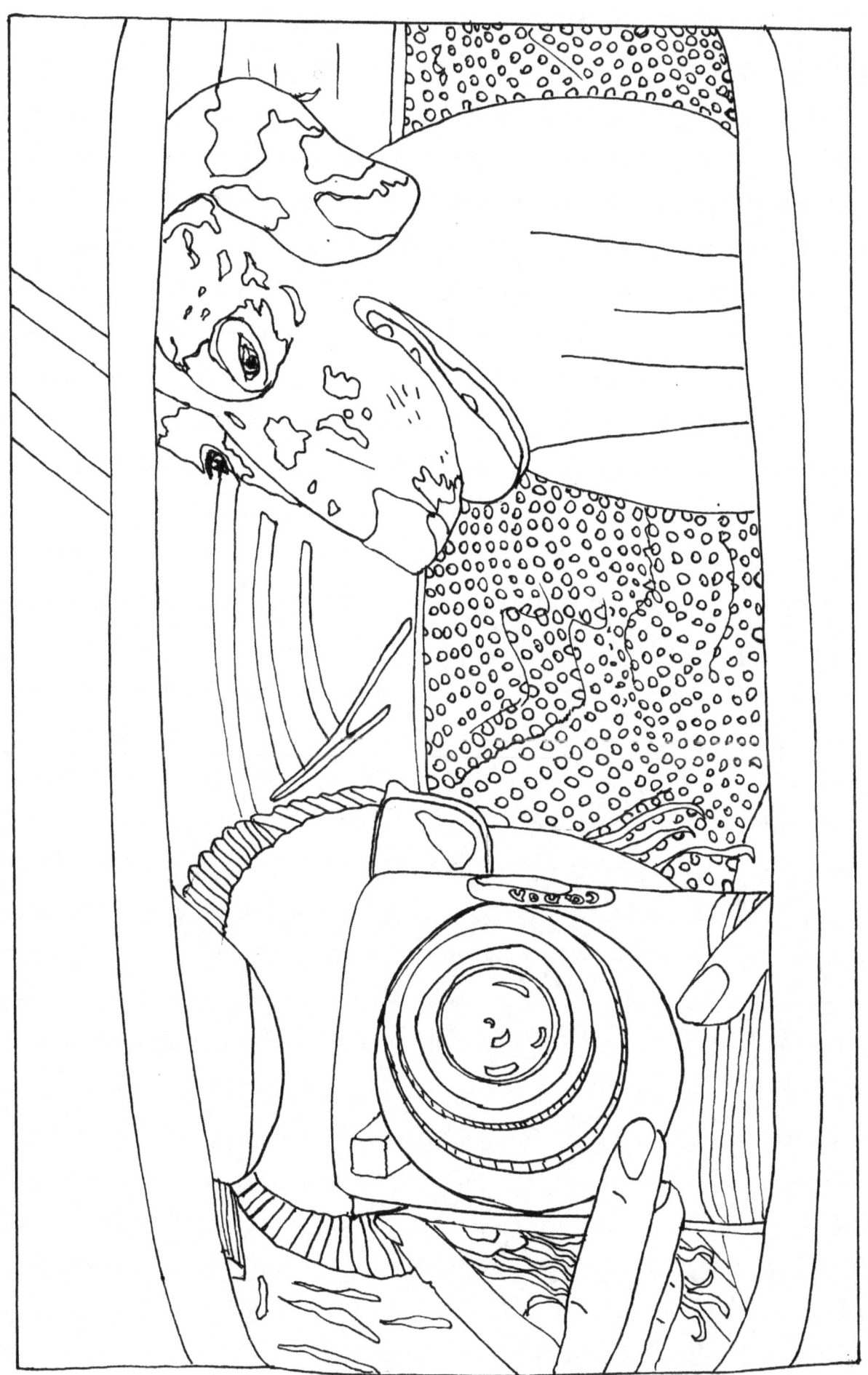

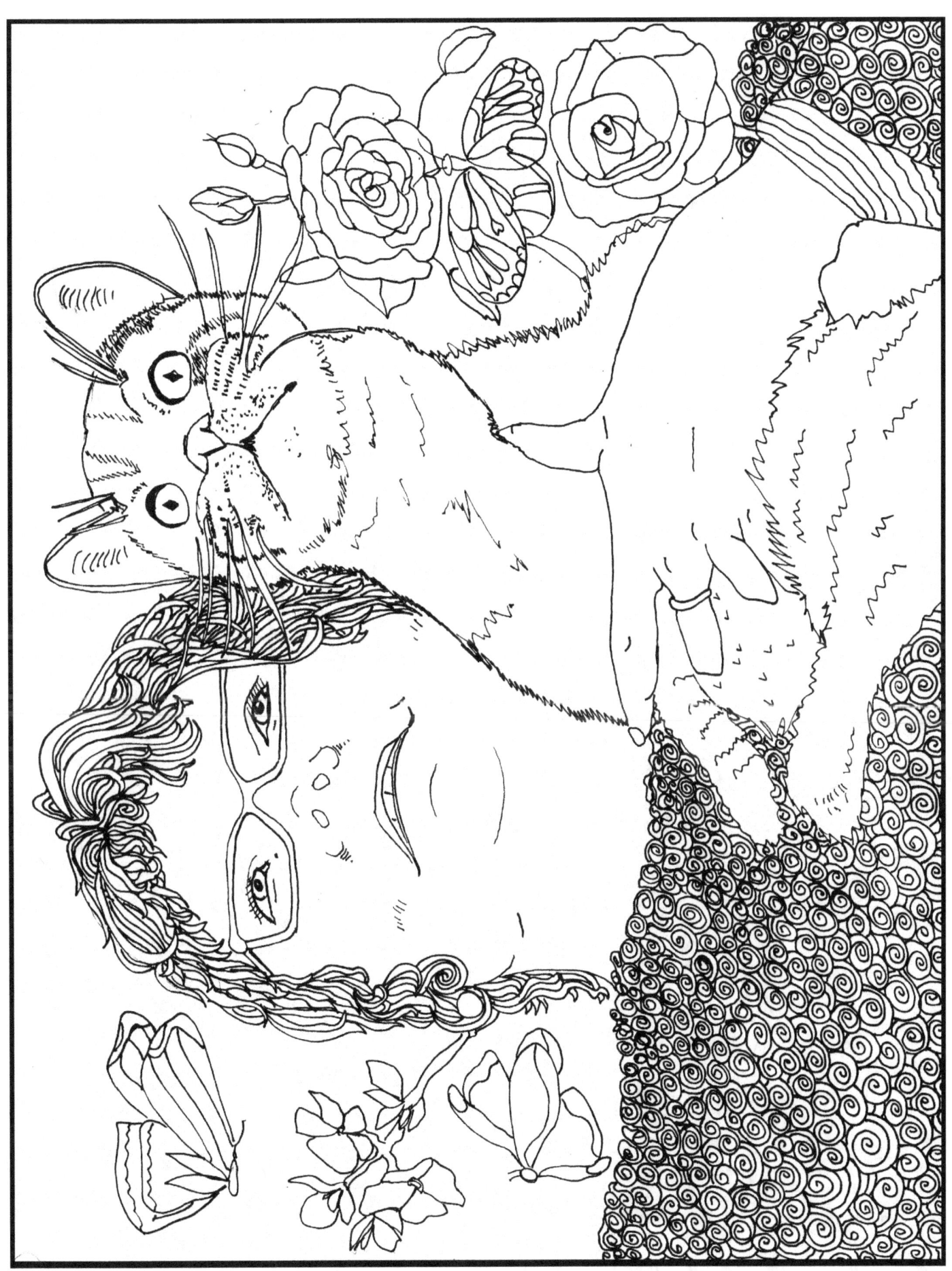

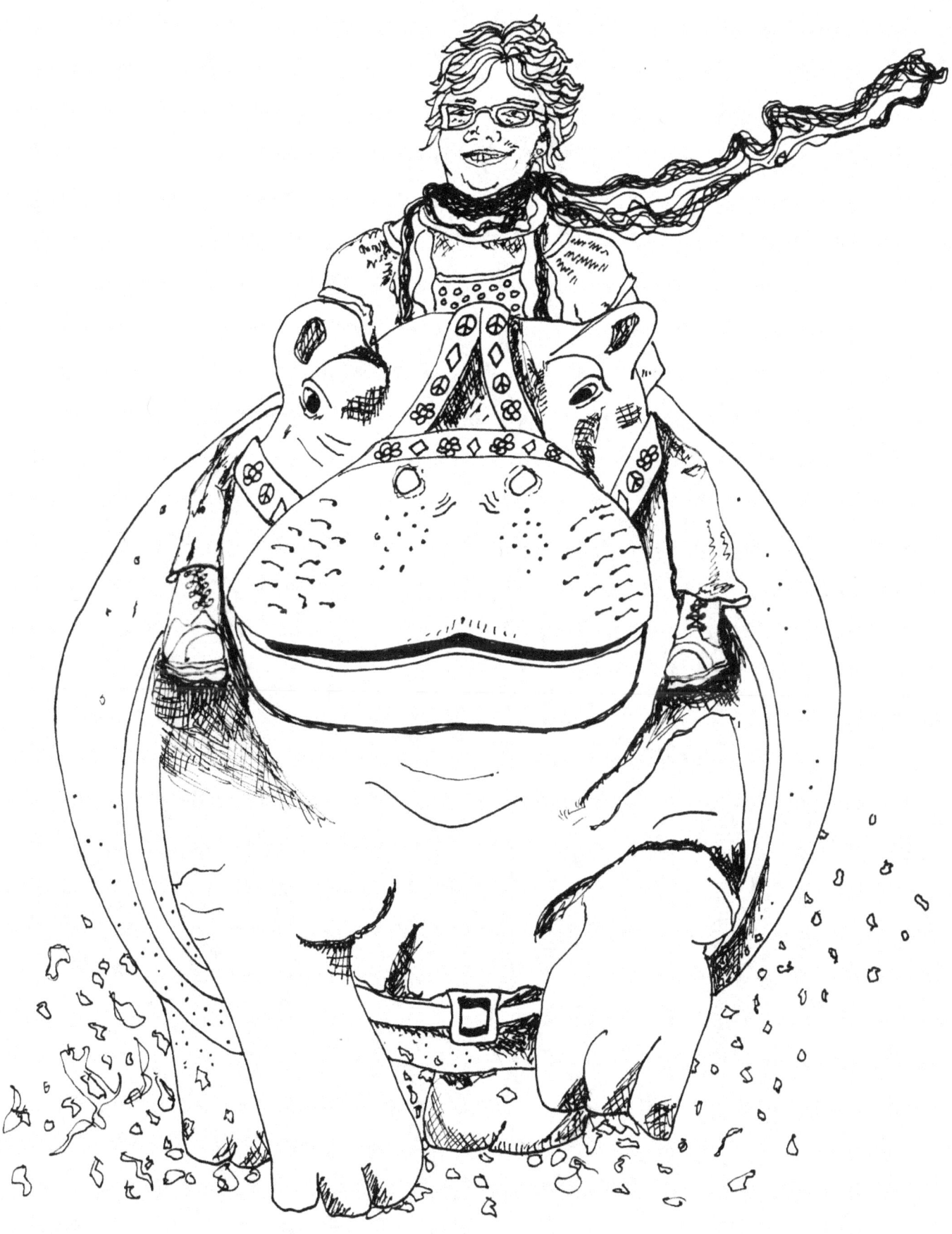

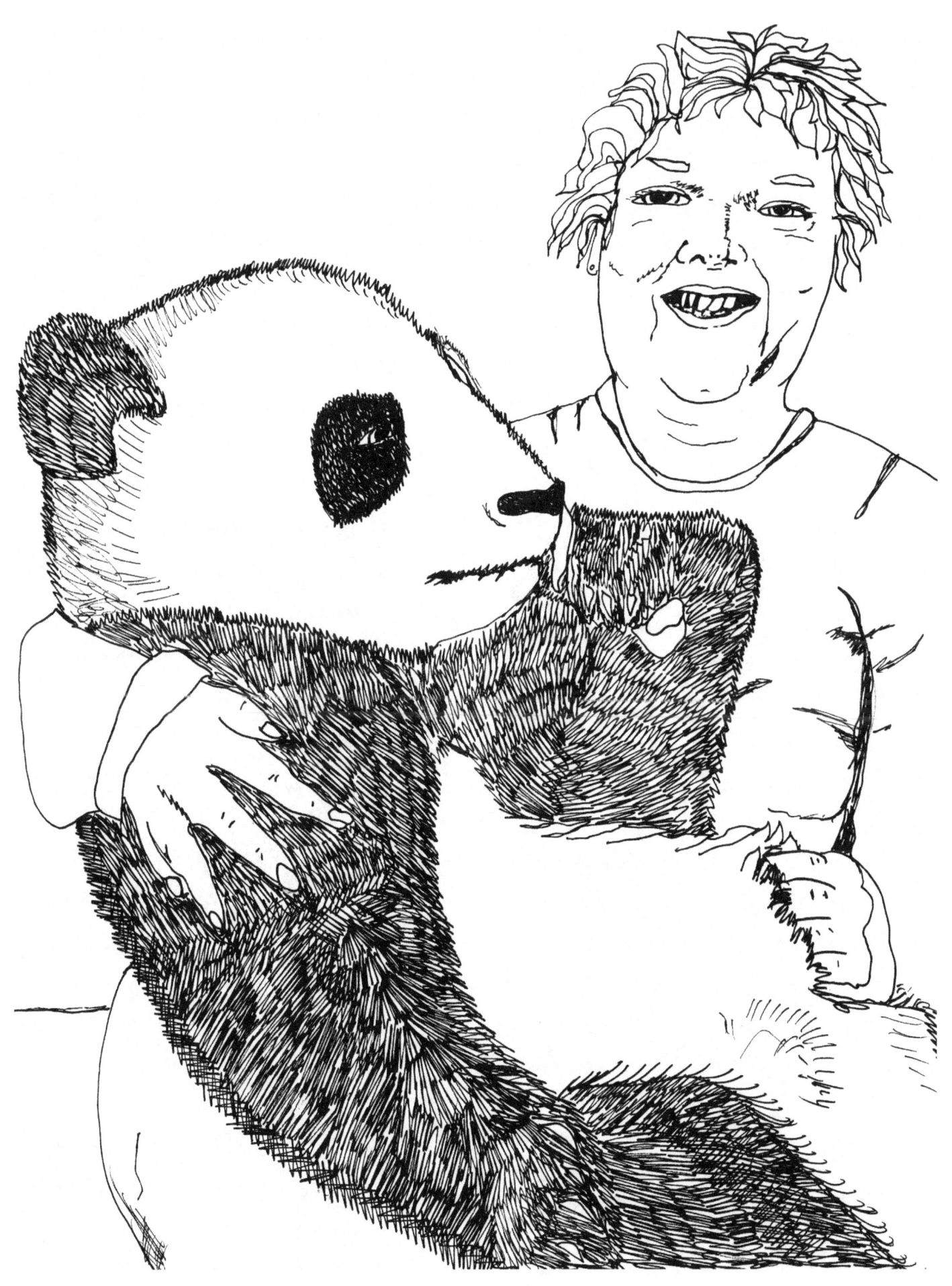

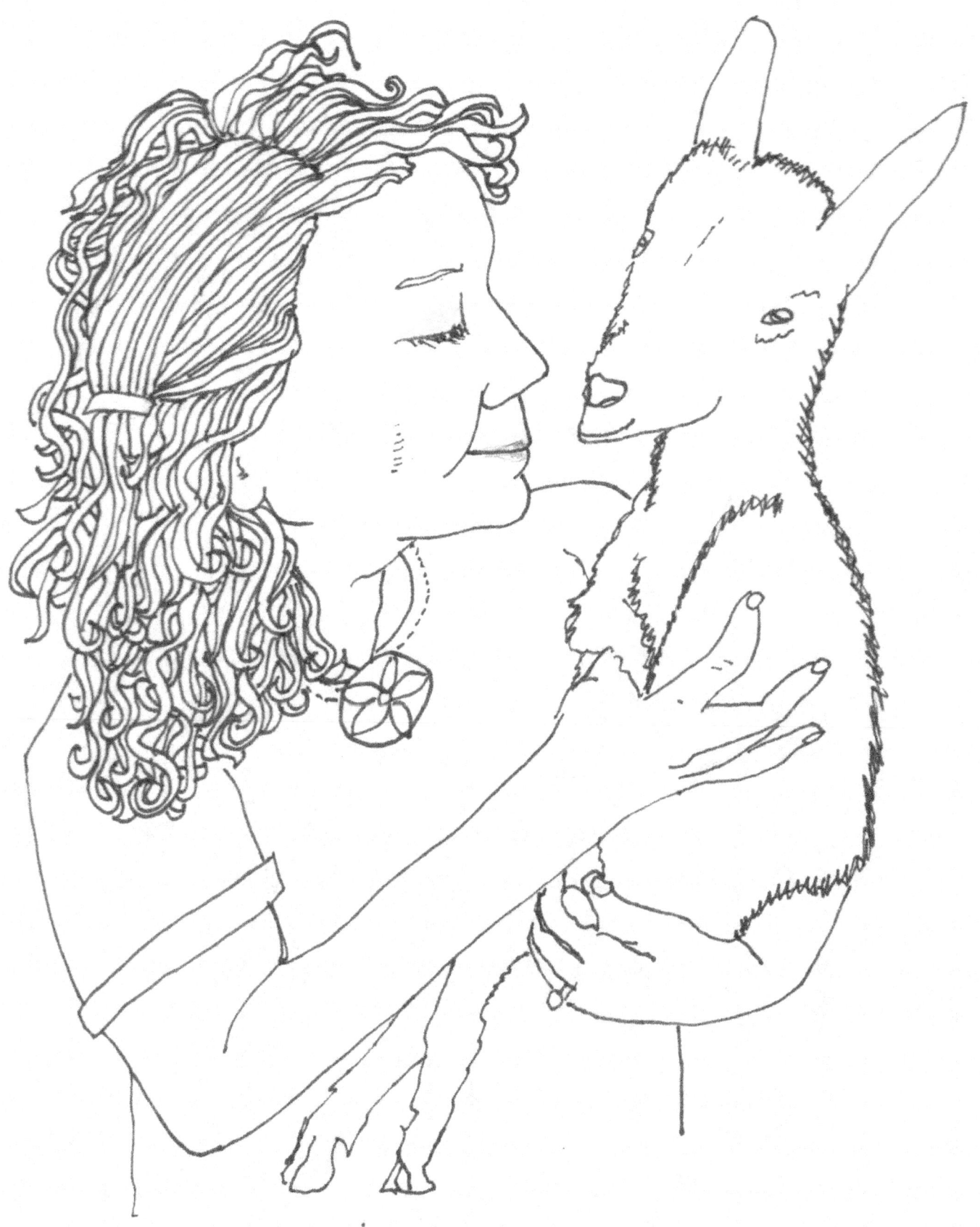

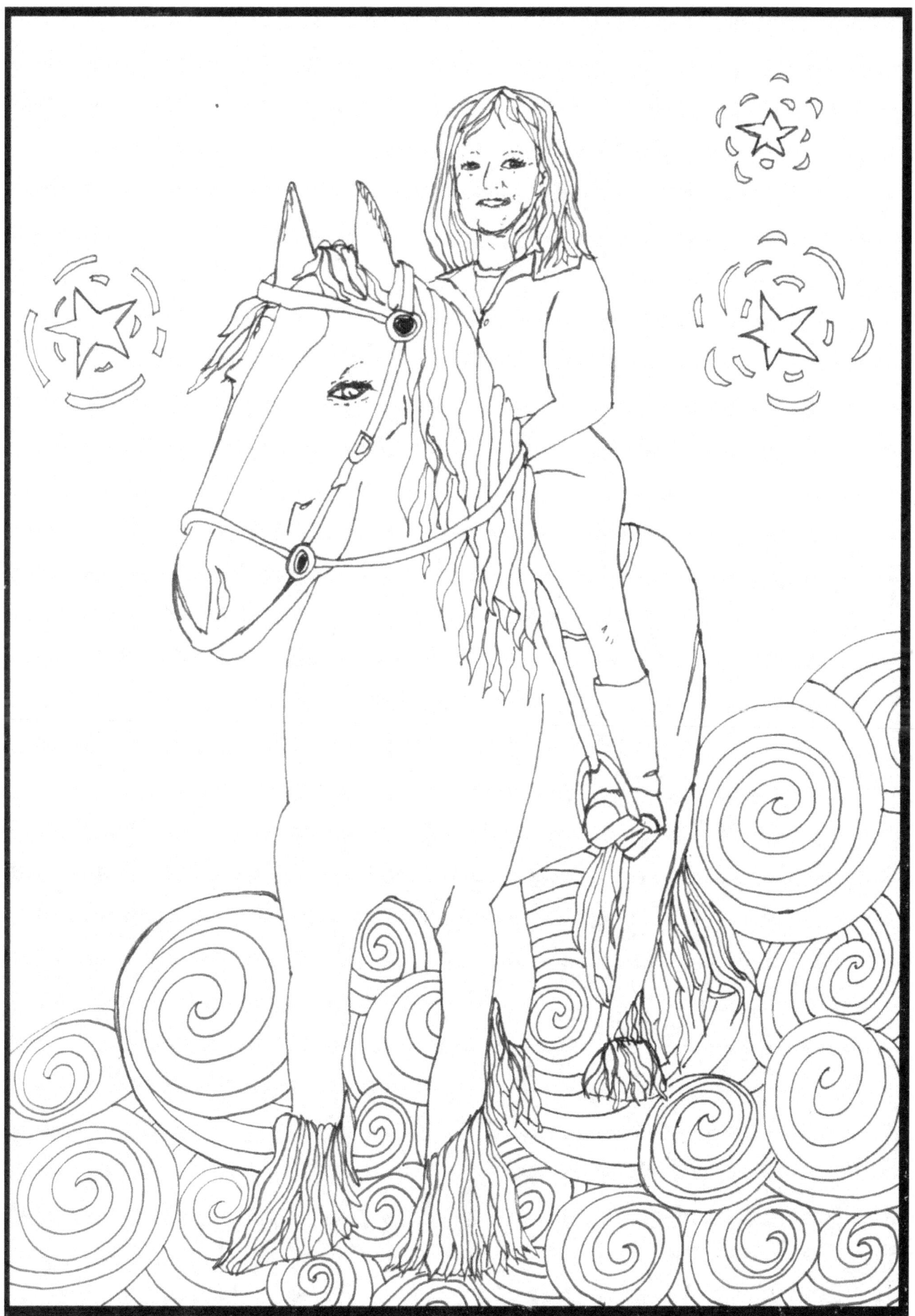

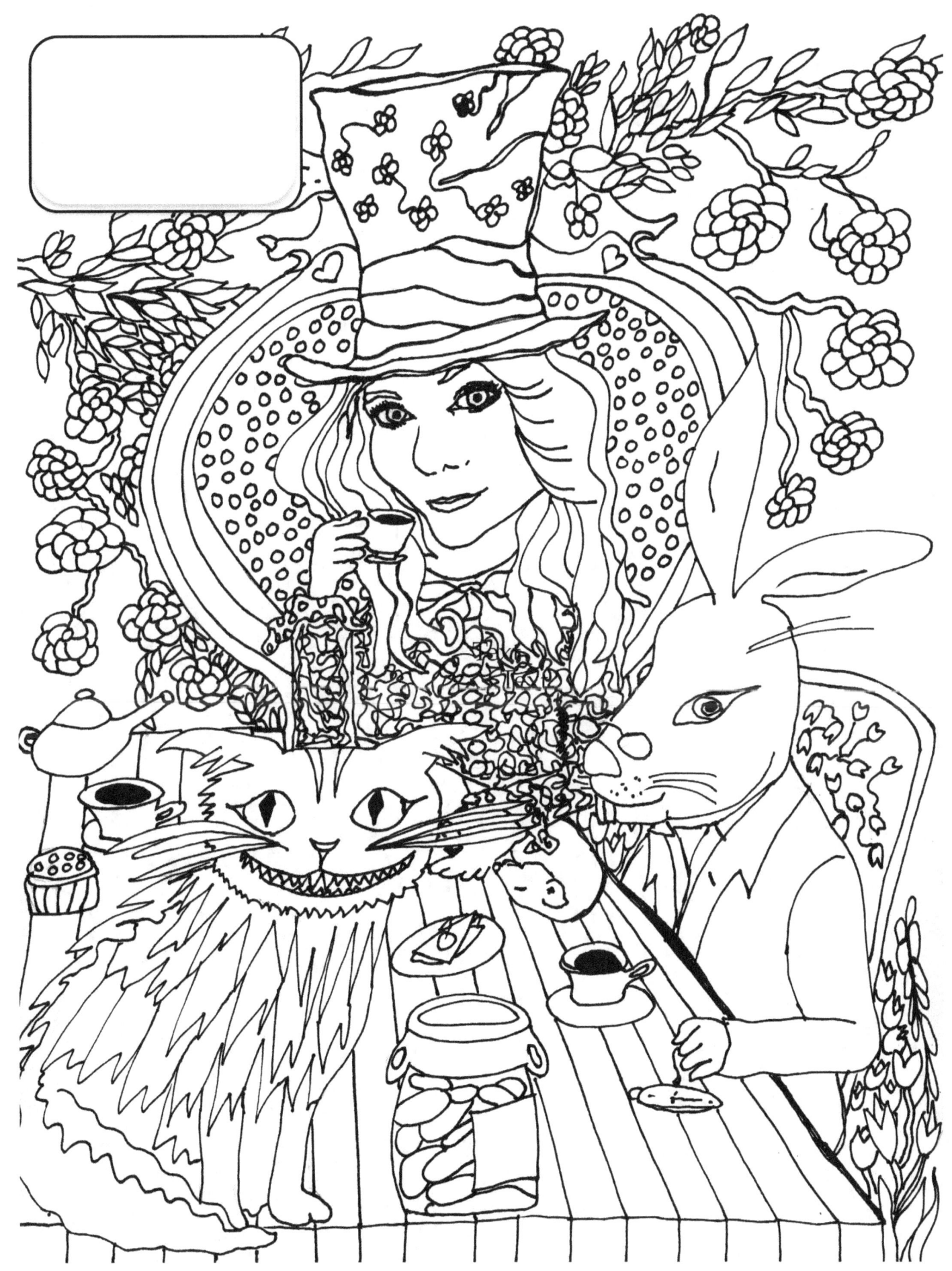

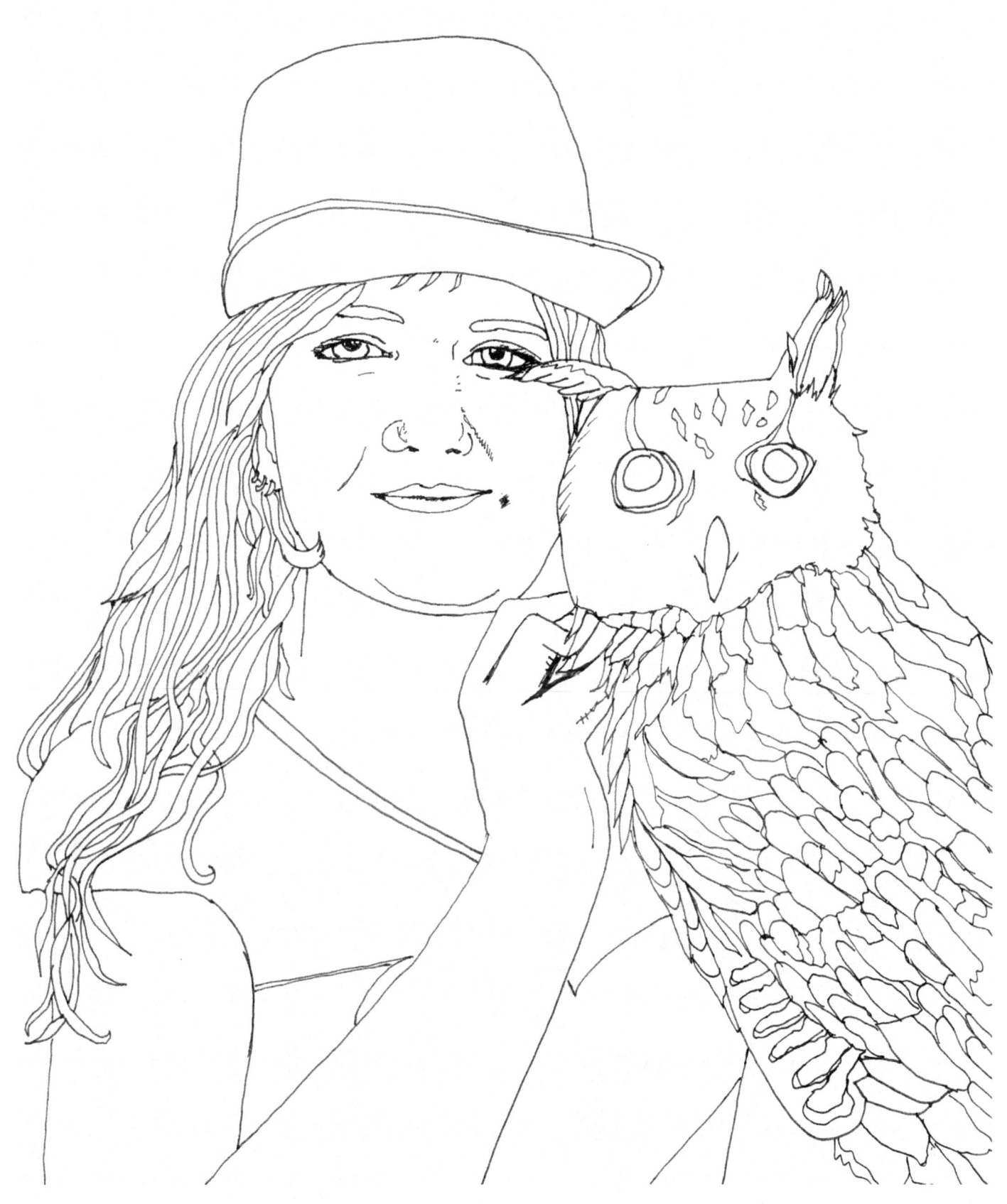

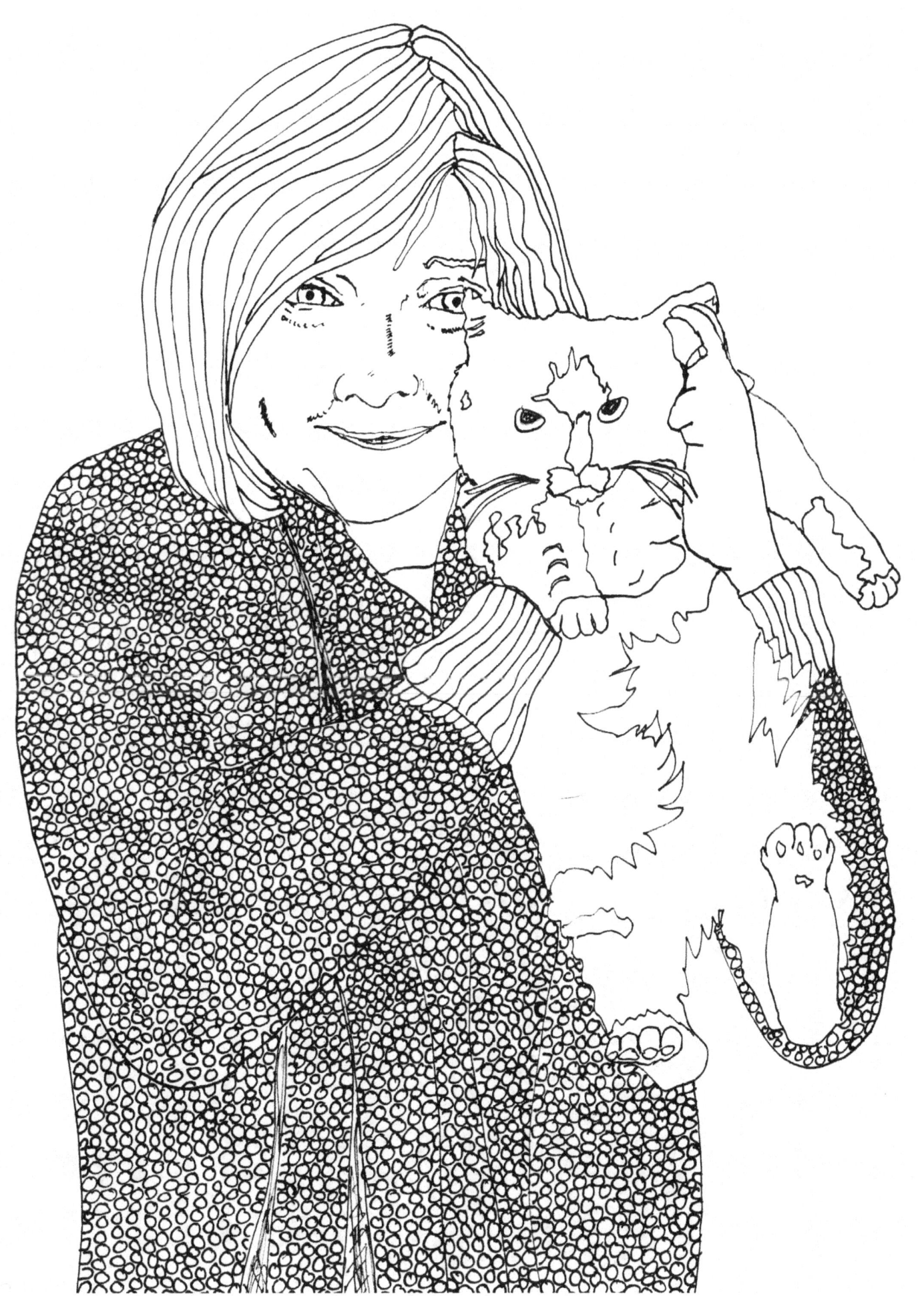

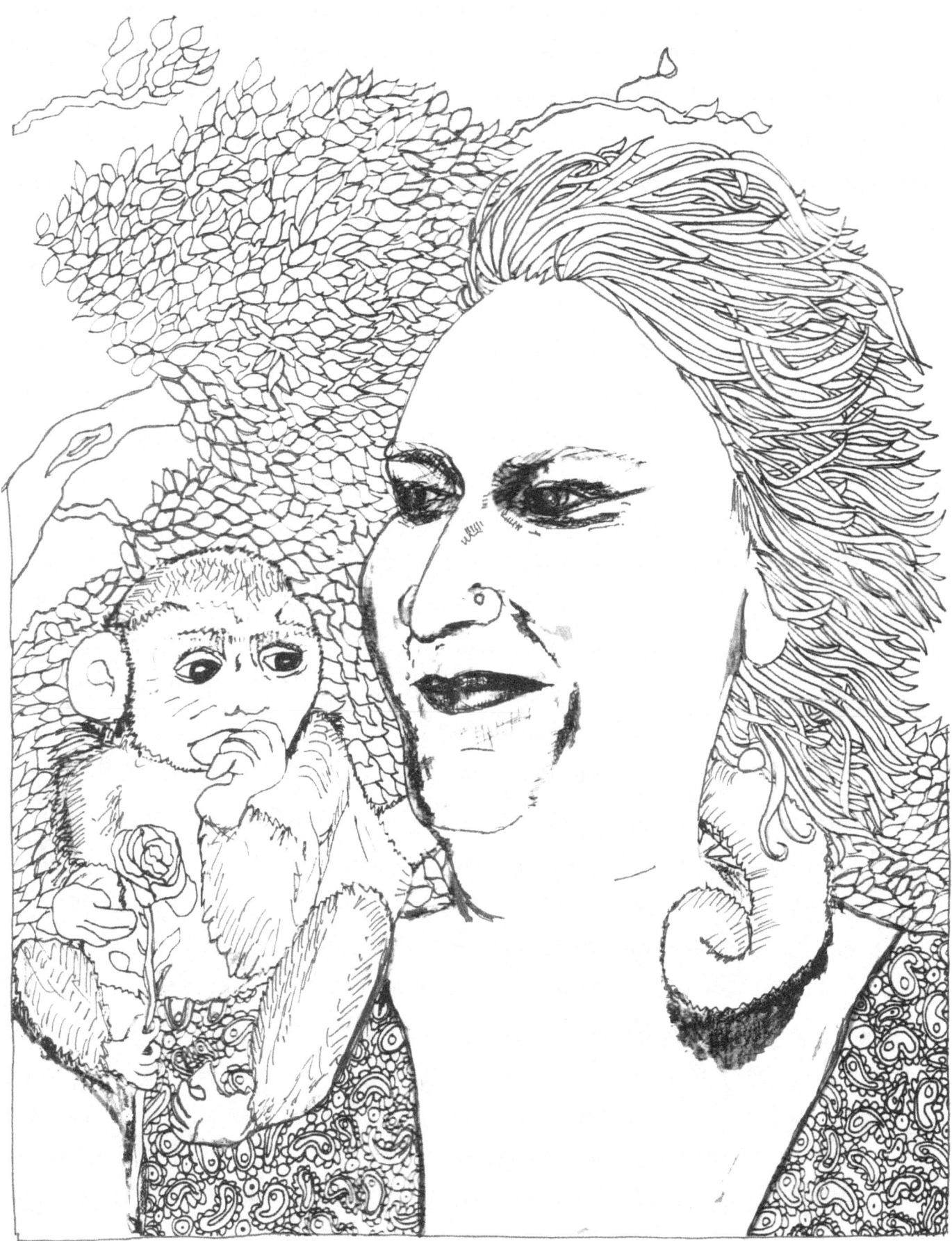

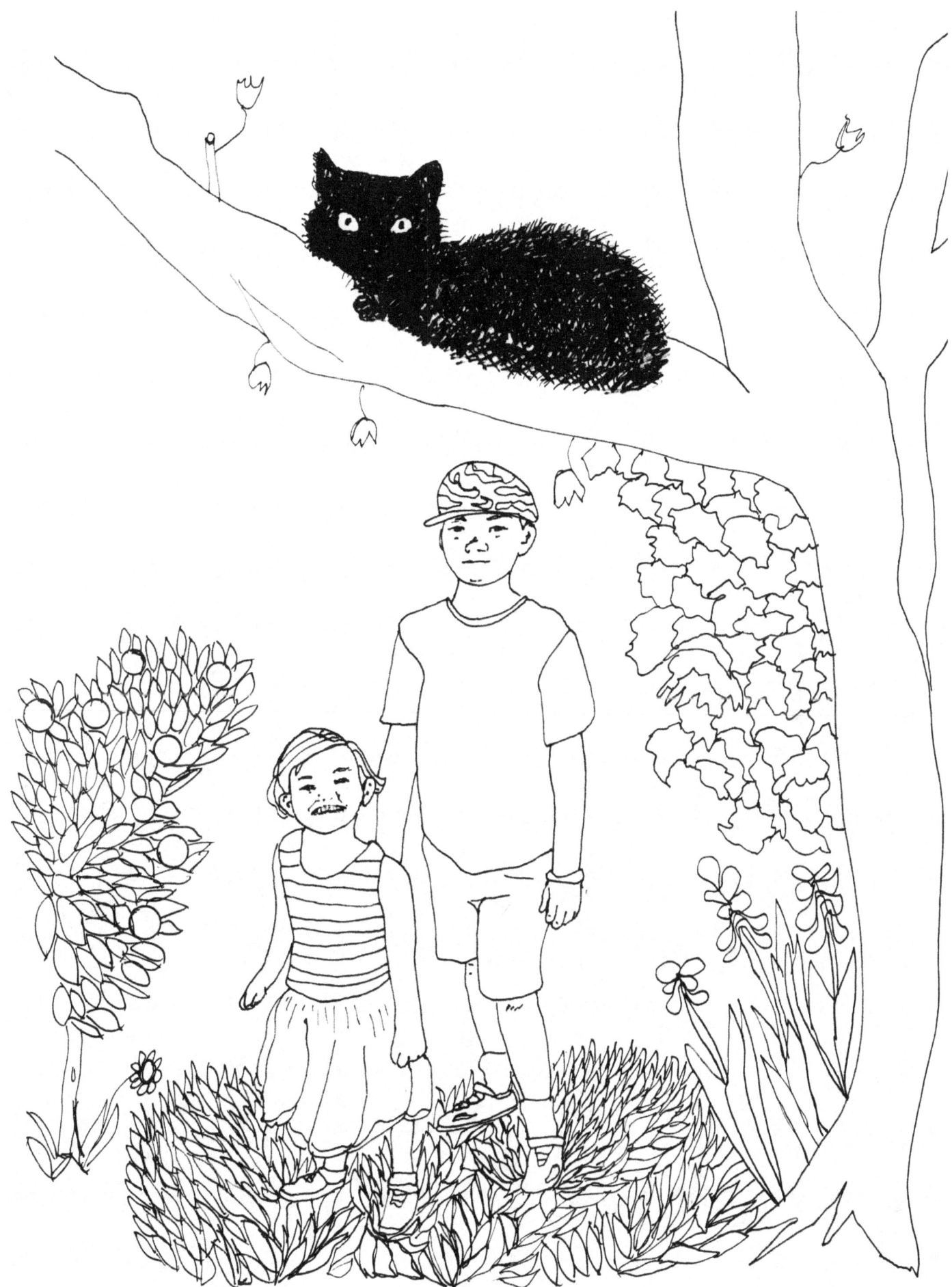

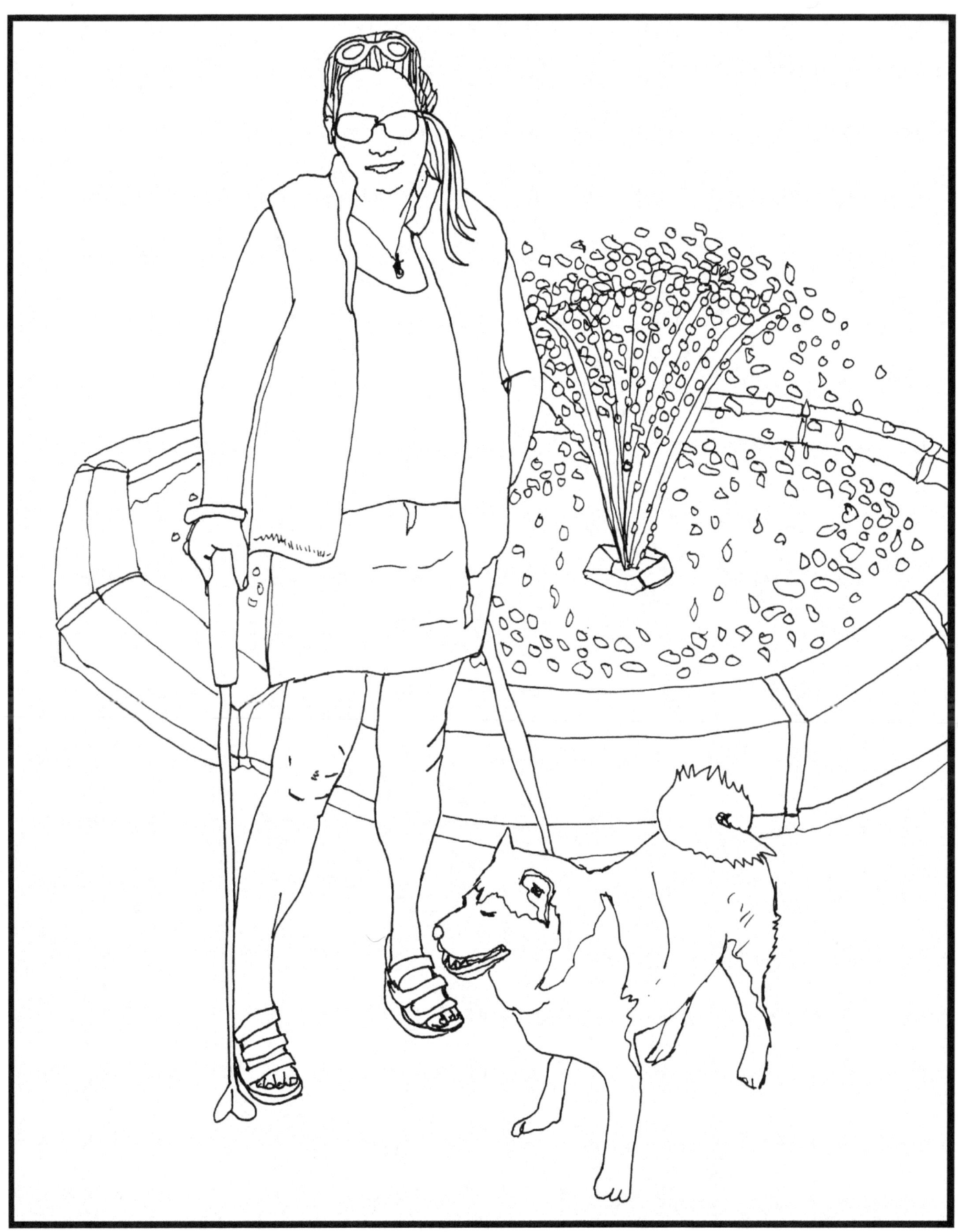

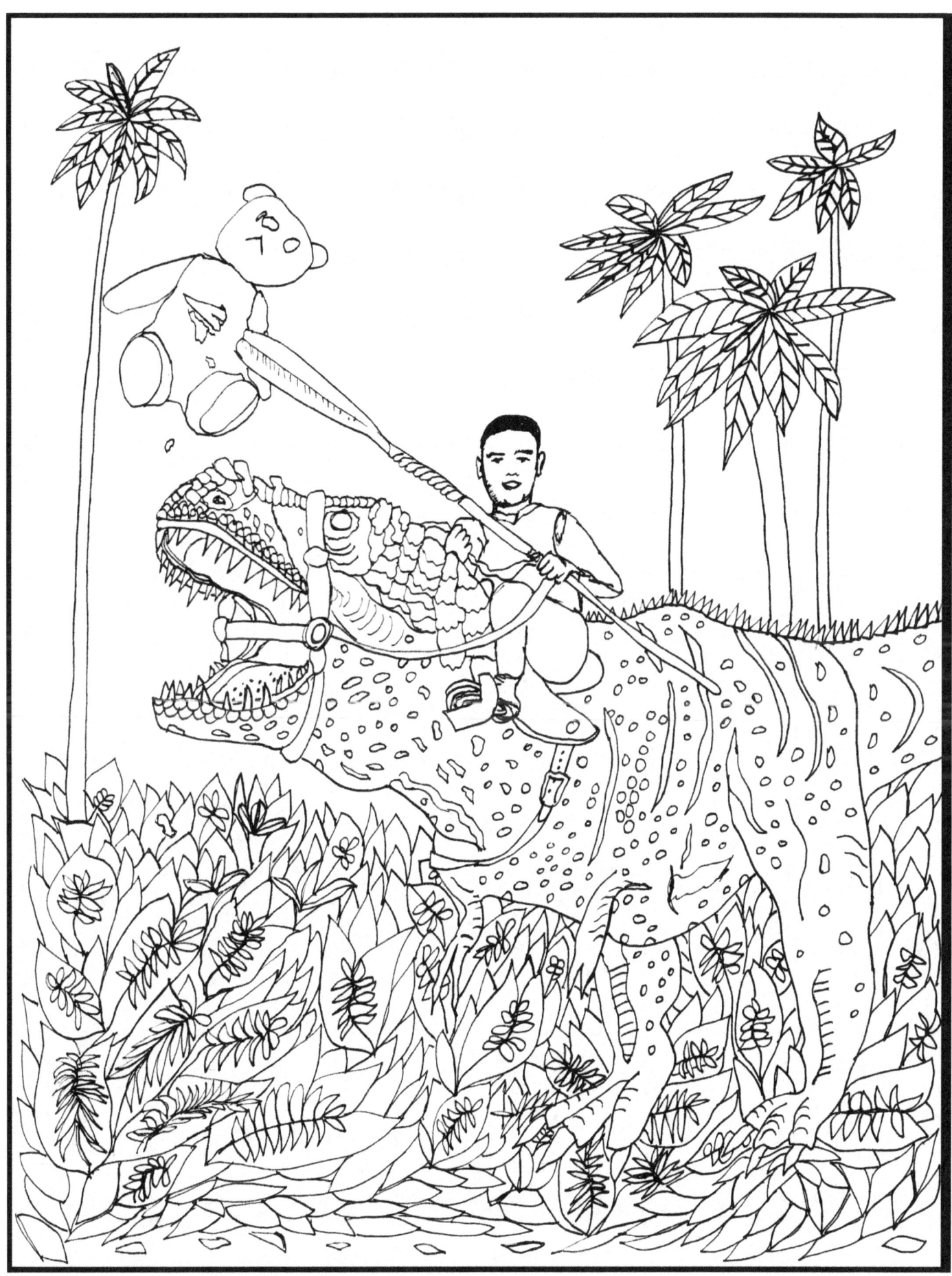

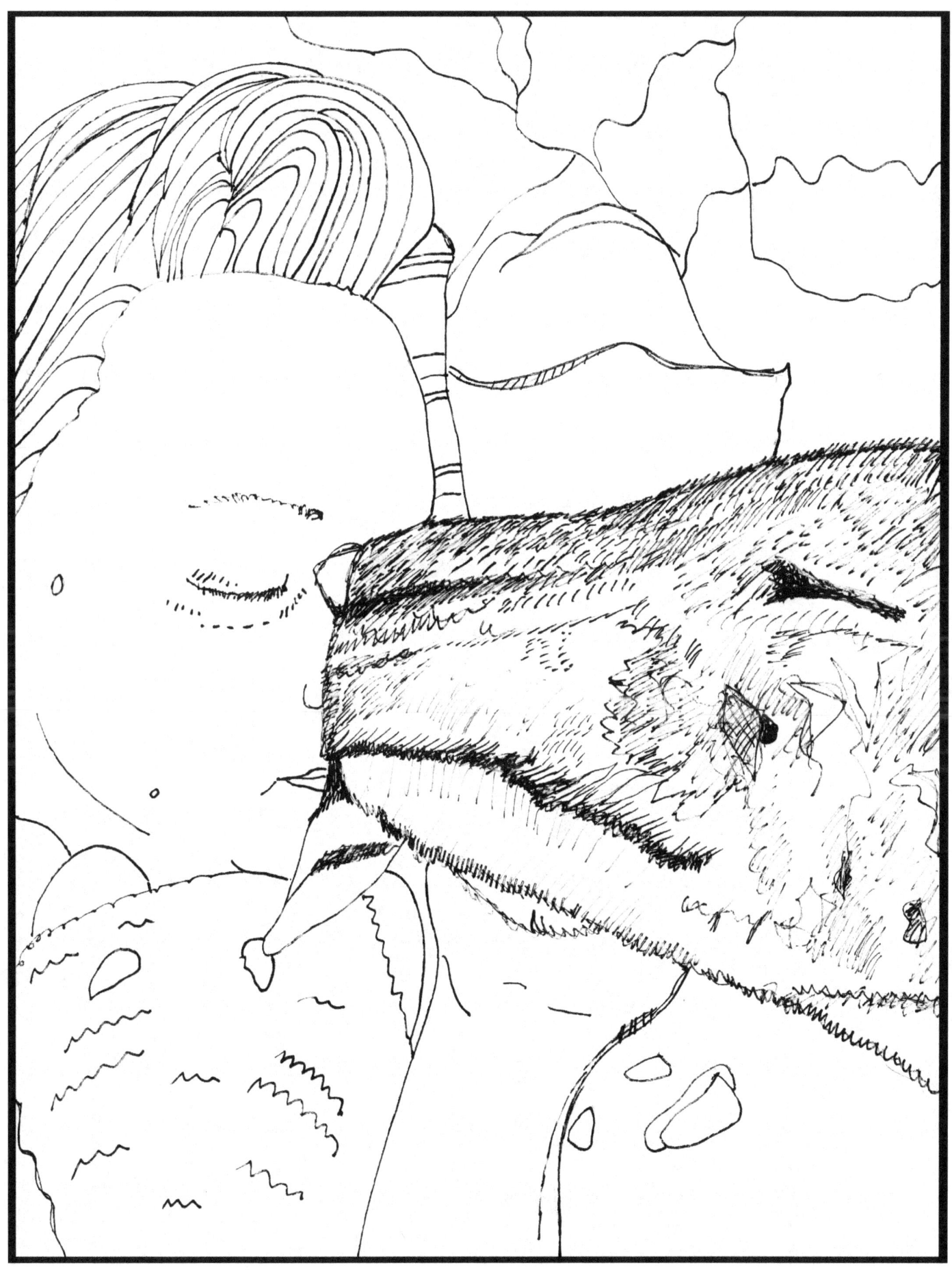

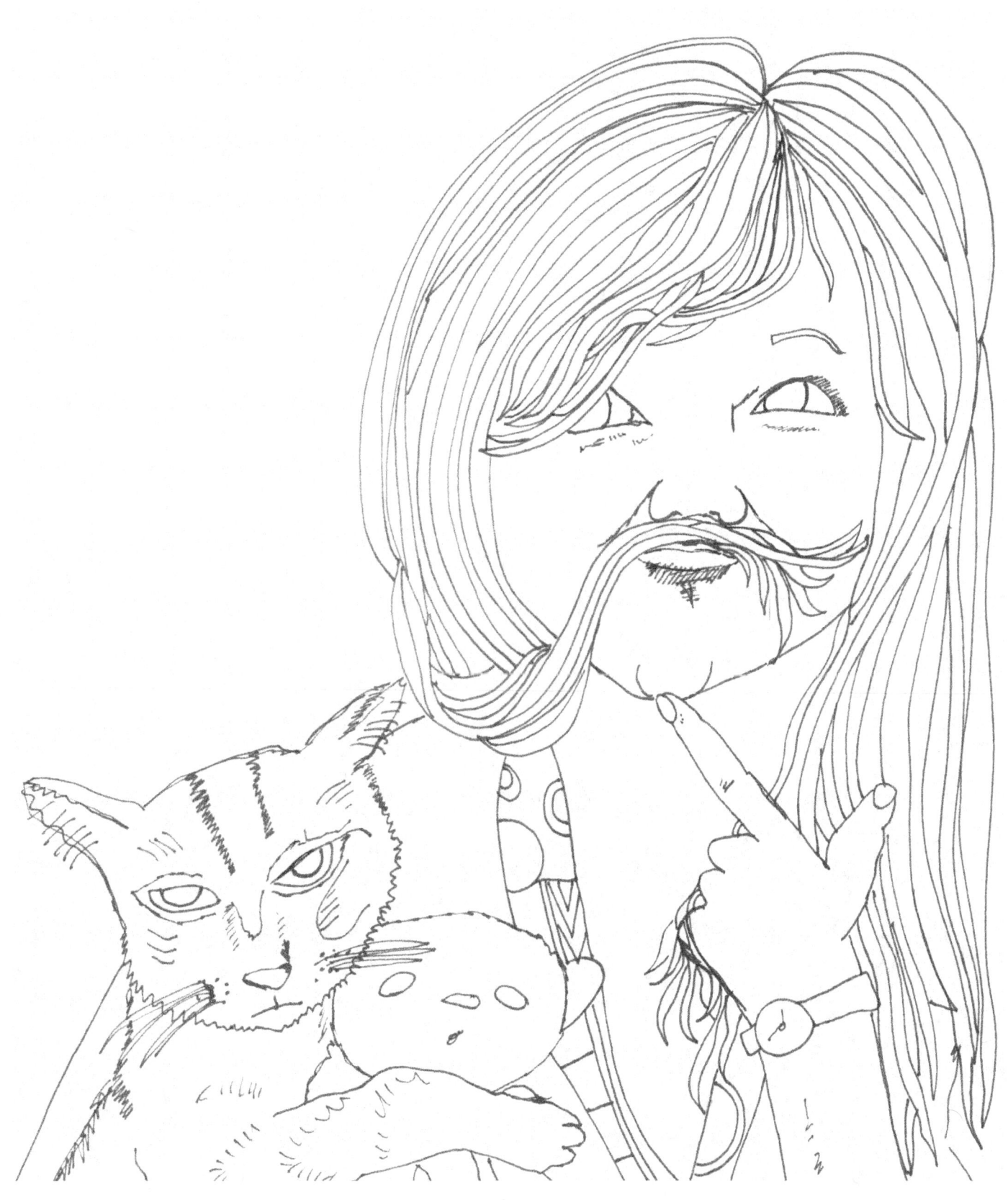

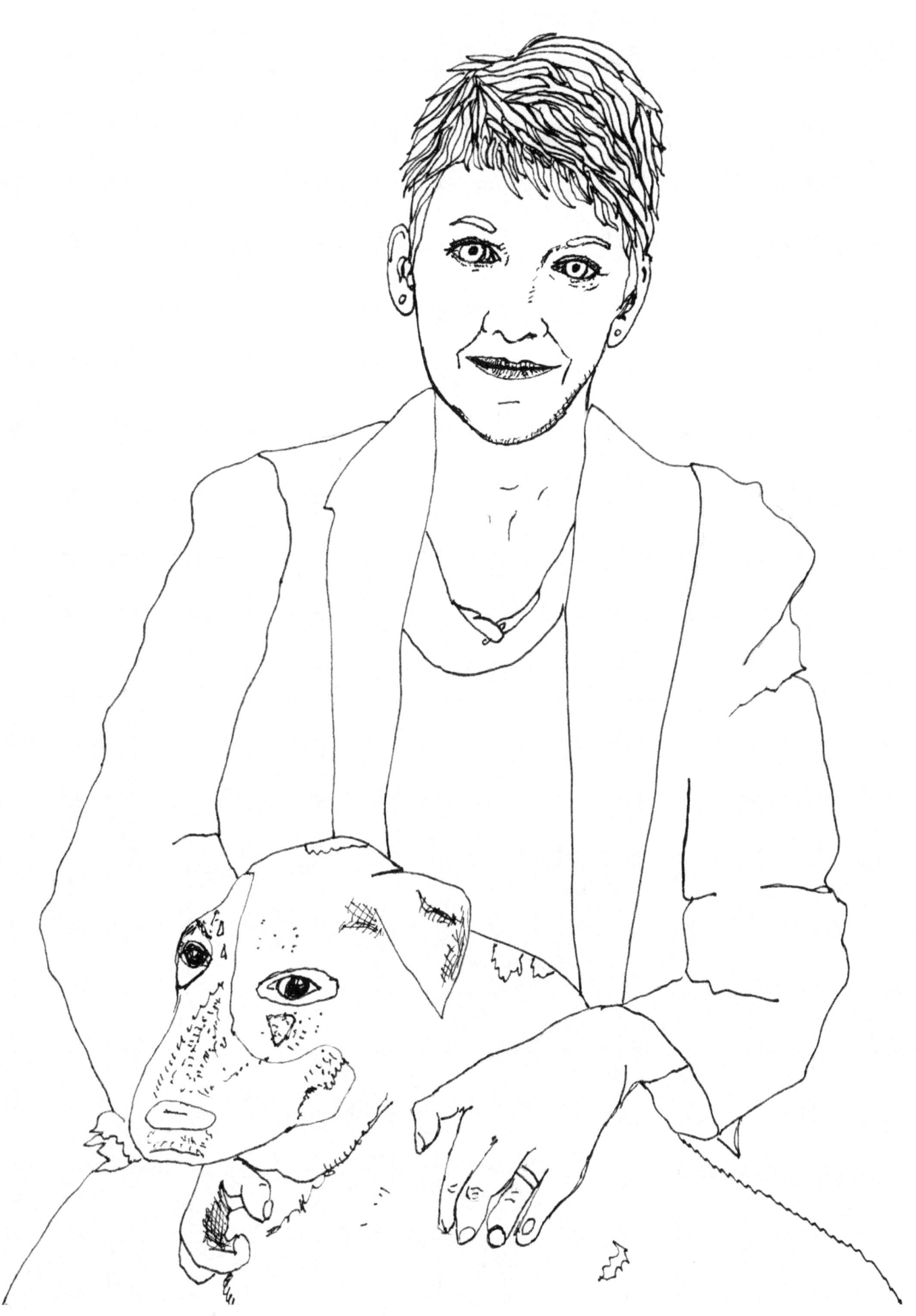

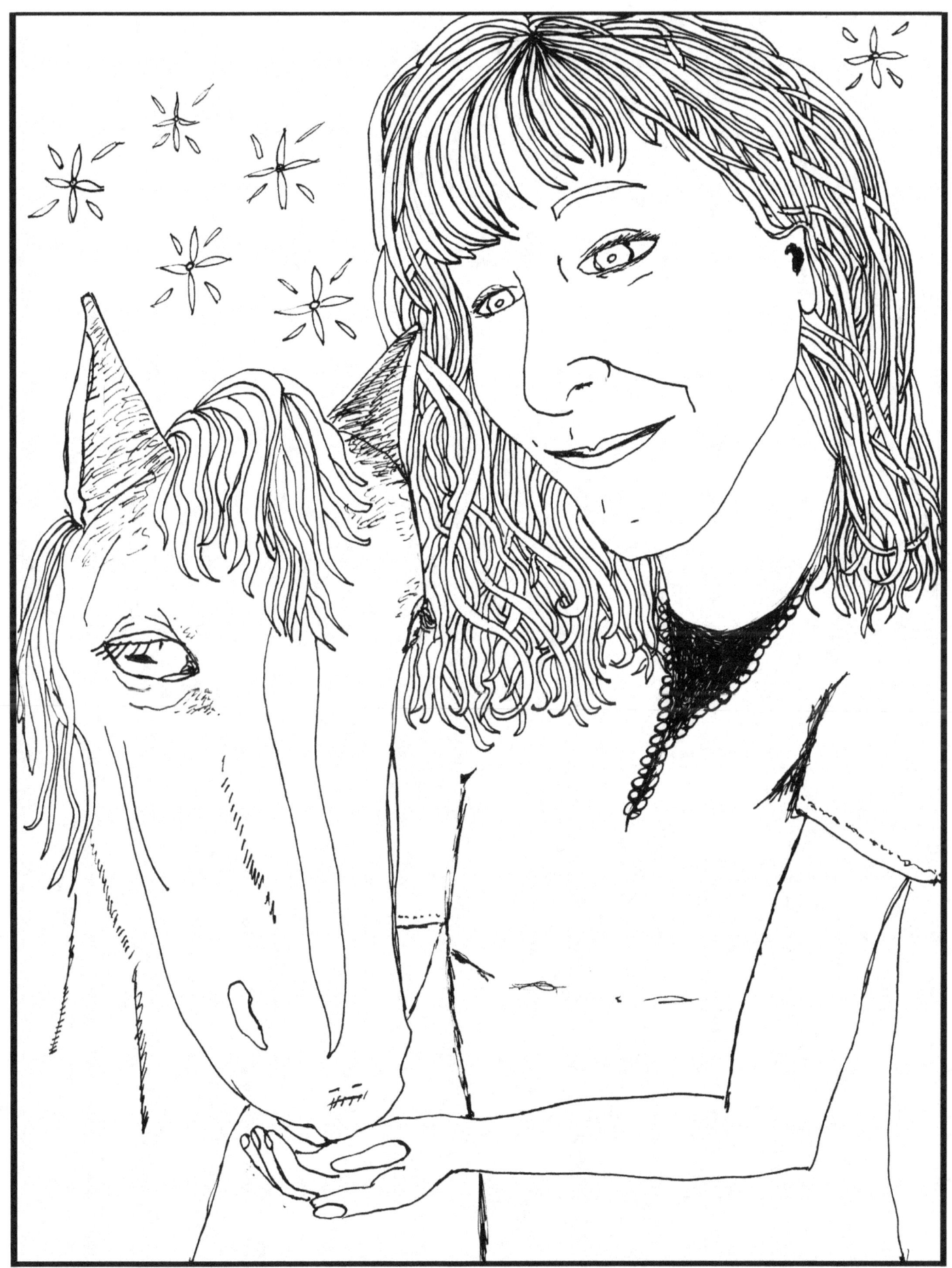

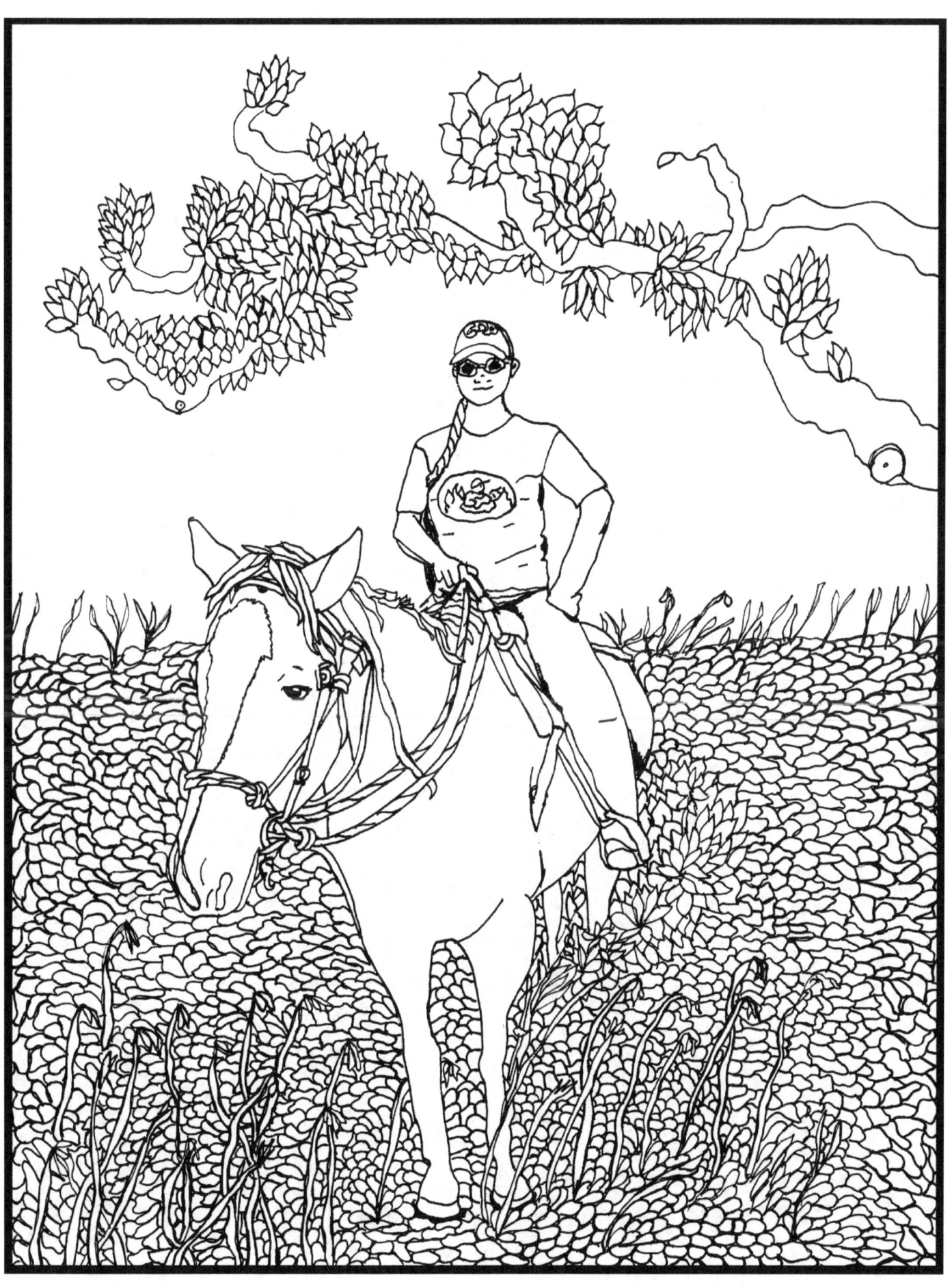

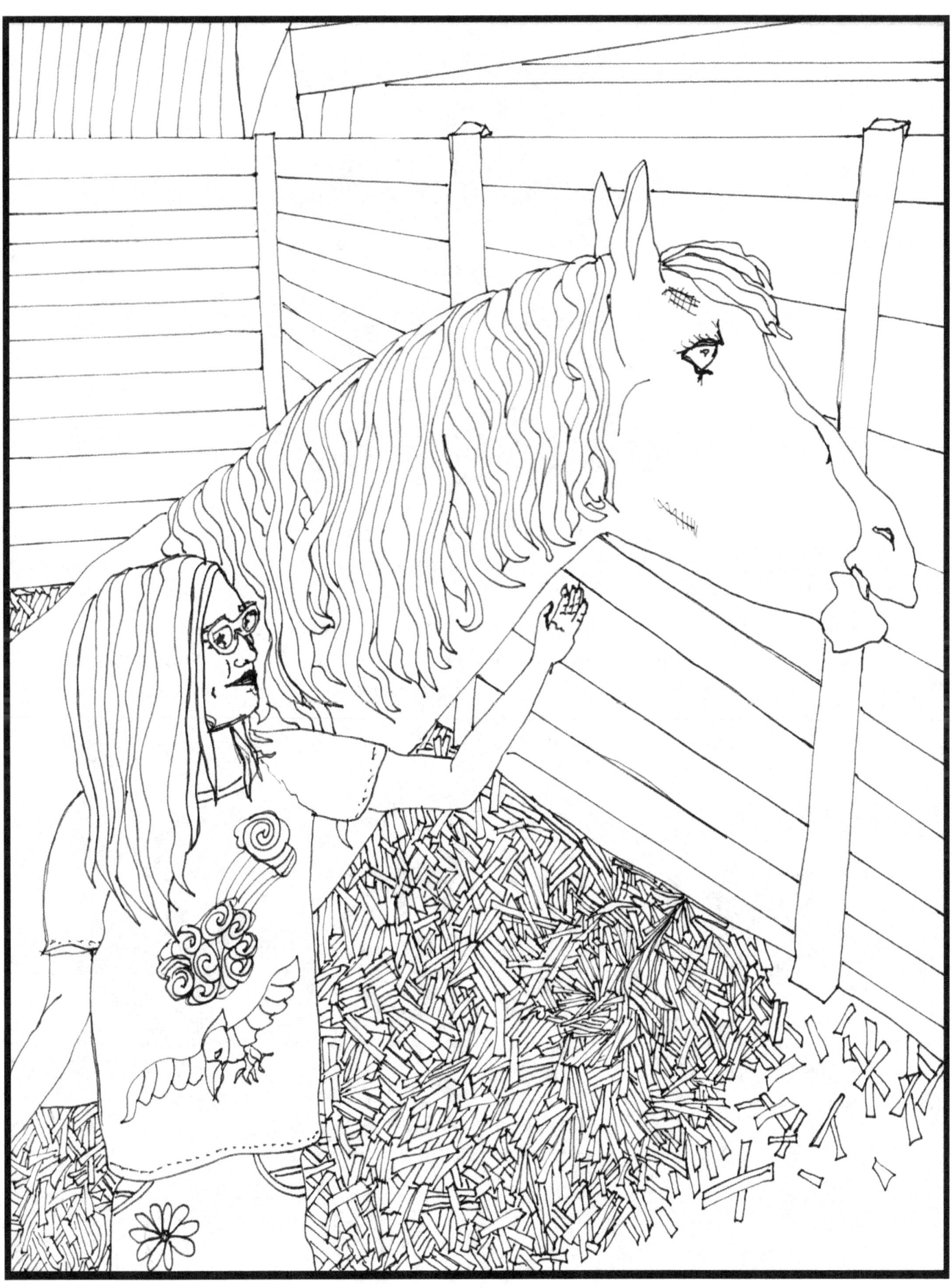

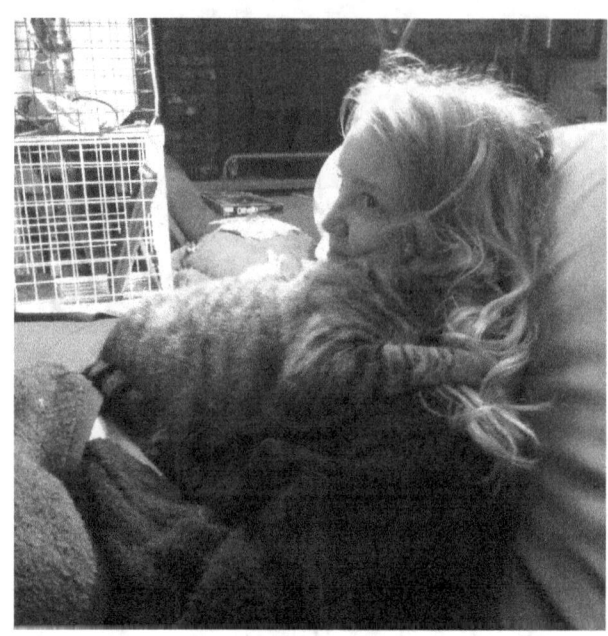

Shoshanah Marohn (Artsy Fartsy Coloring)
and her cat, Tigery

Subscribe to all of her books at: **Patreon.com/Shoshanah**. (Subscribe at the $25 "Love to Color" level before December 21, 2017 and decide what Shoshanah will draw for her next **book**! Visit Patreon.com/Shoshanah for details.)

http://geni.us/Trolls   http://geni.us/Birds   http://geni.us/Birds2

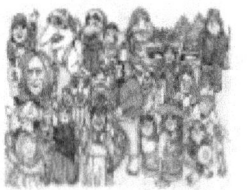 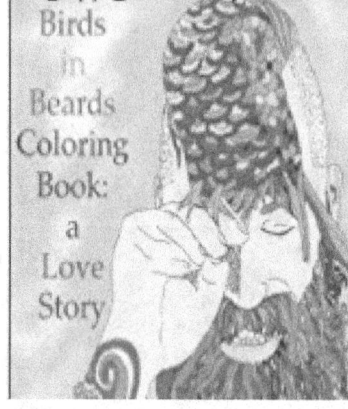 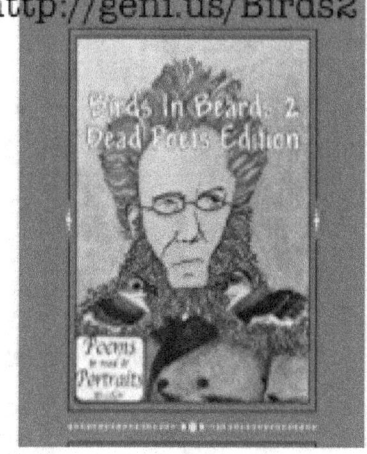

The Trolls of Mount Horeb Coloring Book

The Birds in Beards Coloring Book: A Love Story

Birds in Beards 2 Dead Poets Edition

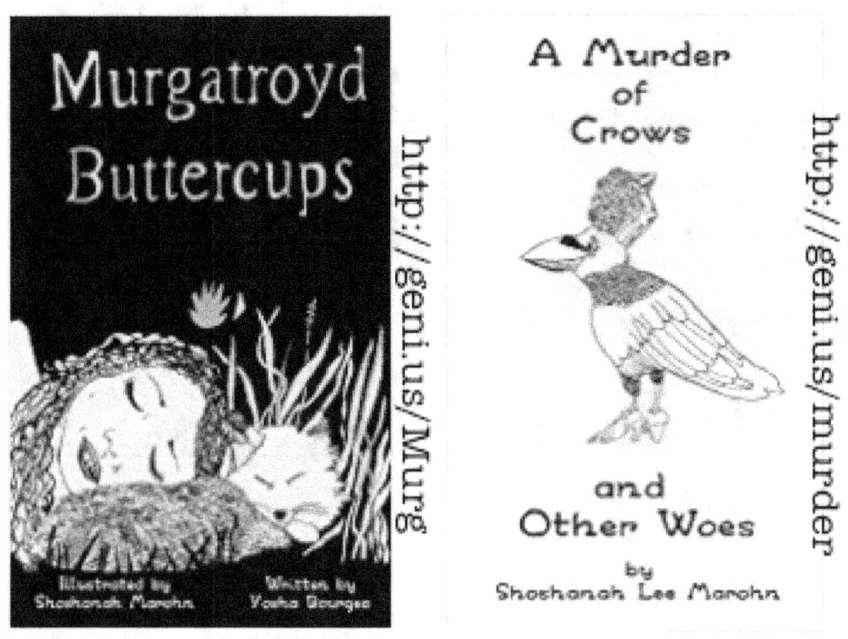

Children's Books Illustrated
By Shoshanah Marohn

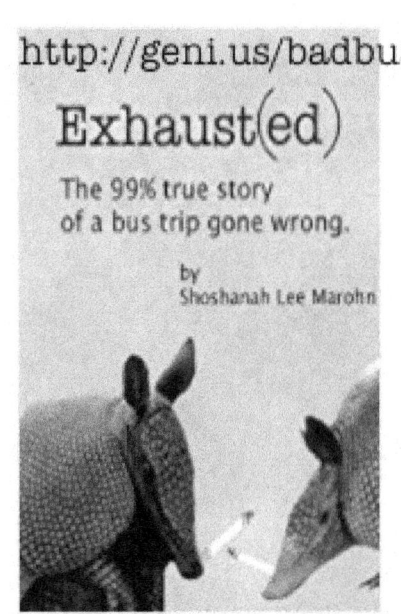

Illustrated Travel Novels: Exhaust(ed) and Avoiding Sex with Frenchmen

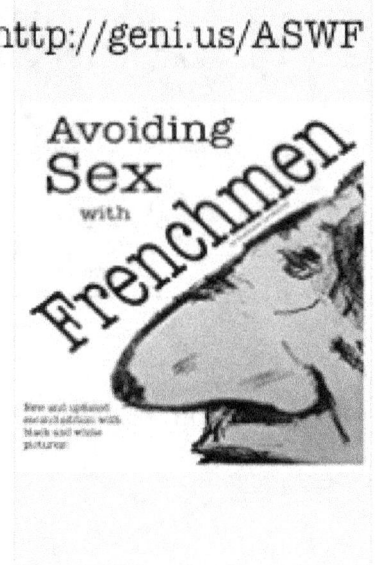

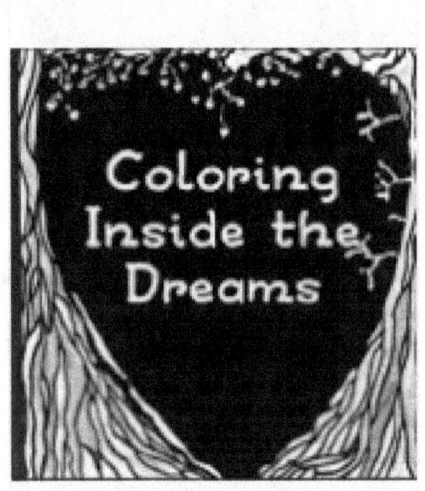

http://geni.us/ColoringDreams

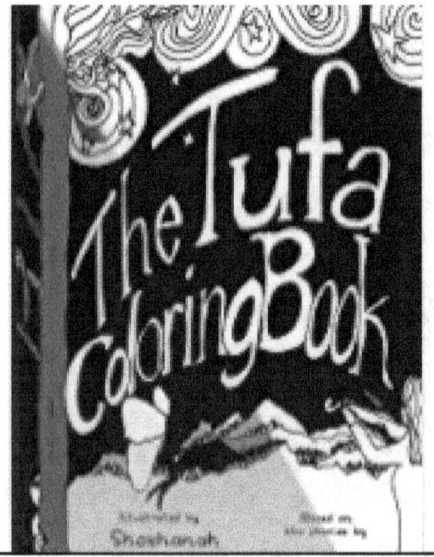

http://geni.us/Tufa

Morbid Mandalas

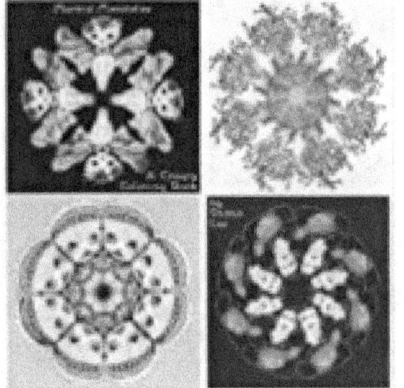

http://geni.us/Morbid

Your Coloring Book Here!

More info at:
http://tinyurl.com/BeBoldwithColor

Contact Shoshanah Marohn at Shoshanah@mhtc.net.

www.ingramcontent.com/pod-product-compliance
Lightning Source LLC
Chambersburg PA
CBHW082220220526
45470CB00010B/3243